P9-CCJ-929

TORONTO
BOOK OF
Everything

Everything you wanted to know about
Toronto and were going to ask anyway

Nate Hendley, Karen Lloyd,
Tanya Gulliver

MACINTYRE PURCELL PUBLISHING INC.

TO OUR READERS

Every effort has been made by authors and editors to ensure that the information enclosed in this book is accurate and up-to-date. We revise and update annually, however, many things can change after a book gets published. If you discover any out-of-date or incorrect information in the Toronto Book of Everything, we would appreciate hearing from you via our website, **www.bookofeverything.com**.

Copyright 2009 by MacIntyre Purcell Publishing Inc.

MacIntyre Purcell Publishing Inc.
232 Lincoln St., PO Box 1142
Lunenburg, Nova Scotia
B0J 2C0 Canada
www.bookofeverything.com
info@bookofeverything.com

Cover photo courtesy of iStock.
Photos: iStock.
Printed and bound in Canada by Transcontinental.
Map courtesy of Tourism Toronto

Library and Archives Canada Cataloguing in Publication
Hendley, Nate
Toronto book of everything / Nate Hendley, Karen Lloyd, Tanya Gulliver.

ISBN 978-0-9784784-0-7
1. Toronto (Ont.). 2. Toronto (Ont.)--Miscellanea. I. Lloyd, Karen
II. Gulliver, Tanya III. Title.

FC3097.3.H46 2009   971.3'541   C2008-905740-6

Introduction

Canada's largest metropolis has both working-class and blueblood roots and now sits firmly in the international cosmopolitan mainstream. Toronto may be the city the rest of the country loves to hate, but those who live there are generally and genuinely fond of it. And, really, why shouldn't we be? Toronto offers choices to satisfy any palate or inclination.

Like great cities everywhere, Toronto is also a product of its contradictions. It was our duty to include as many of them as we could, drawing what we hope is a multi-faceted portrait in tiny increments, a fact or a story at a time.

No one book can really be about everything, of course. As you might expect, our toughest decisions were not what to put in but what to leave out. For every tidbit or profile or anecdote that didn't survive the final trimming, we gave a collective sigh of sorrow and crossed our fingers that it would make the next edition.

As you might expect, *The Toronto Book of Everything* could not have been written without dozens of collaborators and supporters, and so there are a great many people to thank. At the top of the list are the hard-working staff at the City of Toronto Archives. Also a special thank you to our editorial director, Sandy Newton, and to John MacIntyre and Kelly Inglis at the home office.

Others who contributed include Danny Gillis, Gizelle Lau, Wendy Golman, Jane Doucet, and Earl Miller. Finally, our gratitude goes to those whose personal takes on this great city were shoehorned into lists of five at our request—their thoughts and their willingness to share them truly helped us make this book unique.

Tanya Gulliver, Nate Hendley, Karen Lloyd

Table of Contents

Toronto:

A Timeline

About 13,000 years ago: Glaciers retreat from southern Ontario and leave behind large lakes, including Lake Iroquois, which encompasses present-day Lake Ontario.

About 11,700 years ago: Lake Iroquois begins flowing to the sea through the St. Lawrence River rather than down the Hudson, which drops the lake's level and changes its shoreline.

About 10,500 to 11,000 years ago: The first nomadic aboriginals arrive in the Toronto area from the south, following game. The lake level is lower than it is today; the northern shoreline is 20 km further south.

Between 7,000 and 2,000 years ago: Lake Ontario rises and the Scarborough Bluffs begin to erode, creating the current shoreline and eventually leading to the formation of Toronto Island and the harbour.

500 AD: Aboriginal communities grow and become more settled. Populations of about 500 live near each of the large rivers in the Toronto area.

Around 600: Aboriginal people plant corn, beans and squash. Agriculture grows in importance. Over the next 400 years, crop-growing Iroquoian societies in the area gradually become classic longhouse communities.

Late 1500s to early 1600s: The Iroquois move north, and Huron tribes use the area as hunting grounds.

Mid-1600s: The first Europeans, French traders and missionaries, arrive on the north shore of Lake Ontario. Two Seneca villages flourish briefly on the Rouge and Humber rivers.

1720: Sieur Douville builds a small post for fur trading on the Humber River. The French begin to use the word "Toronto" to refer to the area.

1750: French Governor General Jacques-Pierre Taffanel de La Jonquière orders a new fort built to establish a French presence in the area. He calls it Fort Rouillé, but it is also known as Fort Toronto. The fort was abandoned and burned by retreating French forces in 1759. The site is now part of the public lands of Exhibition Place.

1763: New France, which includes Toronto, comes under British rule when the Treaty of Paris concludes the Seven Years' War.

1776: American Independence occurs. An estimated 7,000 United Empire Loyalists make Ontario their new home; about 70,000 more arrive in the following years, lured by cheap land grants.

1787: In the Toronto Purchase, the First Nations people, the Mississaugas, sell 250,808 acres of land to the British for just over a dollar per acre. The price includes 149 barrels of goods and a small amount of cash, with a total value of 1,700 British pounds, or about $235,000 in today's Canadian dollars. The goods included 2,000 gun flints, 24 brass kettles, 10 dozen mirrors, two dozen laced hats, a bale of flowered flannel and 96 gallons of rum.

1793: Upper Canada's Lieutenant-Governor John Graves Simcoe founds the Town of York at Toronto and shifts the province's capital there. A fort is built to defend the fledgling town against American invasion.

1794: Scadding Cabin is built by the Queen's York Rangers on behalf of John Scadding, who served John Graves Simcoe. Today it is the oldest building in Toronto and now located adjacent to the Fort Rouillé Monument on the western Canadian National Exhibition grounds.

1794: John Graves Simcoe Wright is the first white child born in York. His father, a retired soldier in the Queen's Rangers, clearly demonstrates his respect for the lieutenant-governor.

1797: Upper Canada's first session of Parliament held in York begins on June 1 in new buildings close to what is now the intersection of Parliament and Front streets.

1798: Toronto's first jail and hanging yard are built on King Street East at Leader Lane. The first hanging occurs on Oct. 11.

1803: Governor Peter Hunter designates 5.5 acres of land south of King Street, between Jarvis and Church, as "the Marketplace." On market day, Saturday, other stores cannot sell goods found at the market.

1807: York's first church opens. The congregation has already been meeting for 10 years in government buildings. Henry Queeton builds the first brick house in York on the northeast corner of King and Frederick streets.

1813: During the War of 1812, which ends three years later, York is occupied by American troops for six days in April. Buildings are looted and burned, including those of Parliament. American troops gain hold again for two days in July.

1816: Steamships begin to ply the waters of Lake Ontario, expanding York's role as a port.

Bio John Graves Simcoe

As every good Toronto schoolchild knows, the city's founding father was John Graves Simcoe, Upper Canada's first lieutenant-governor and a man who disliked the settlement's un-British name so much that he changed Toronto to York.

Simcoe first established Upper Canada's civic government in Niagara in 1792. A year later, concerned that the town was vulnerable to American attack, he shifted operations to Toronto, then an isolated piece of hinterland on the north shores of Lake Ontario. Simcoe quickly set up a generous system of free land grants aimed at attracting Americans. He drove roads west to Hamilton (Dundas Street) and north into the wilderness (Yonge Street). He also promoted a range of enterprises, from hat making to mining.

Although Simcoe's stay in Canada only lasted four years, his decisions and approach to life and duty had a significant impact on the future City of Toronto. His only Canadian-born daughter, Katherine, died in York (he had four other daughters and a son). She is buried in the Victoria Square Memorial Park on Portland Avenue. "Castle Frank" (named after the Simcoe's young son, Francis) was the tongue-in-cheek name given to their log cabin, which was replete with four large tree trunks passing for classical columns (Castle Frank was located in what is now the eastern part of Cabbagetown). The diary of Simcoe's wife, Elizabeth, has been invaluable to researchers and historians of early York and Upper Canada.

Simcoe left the fledgling capital in 1796 and lived only another 10 years. His legacy—promoting industry and establishing a British beachhead on the north shore of Lake Ontario—continued to inspire those he left behind. In 1903 his place in the city's history was honoured by the unveiling of the General John Graves Simcoe monument at Queen's Park in Toronto.

1829: The Methodist Church establishes Canada's first publishing company in Toronto: the Methodist Book and Publishing House. Renamed Ryerson Press in 1919 after its founder, Egerton Ryerson; it becomes McGraw-Hill Ryerson following a 1970s buyout and merger.

1830: Upper Canada College, an elite private school for boys, is founded. The York Mechanics' Institute also forms, establishing a reference and circulating library to educate workers.

1832: A cholera outbreak results 205 deaths (another outbreak occurs in 1834).

1834: York officially becomes Toronto again when the town is incorporated as a city. The population is 9,254.

1837: Thornton Blackburn, an escaped Kentucky slave, establishes the city's first cab business. He hears about the available hackney cab while waiting on the city's legal elite in Benchers' Dining Room at Osgoode Hall. His red-and-yellow cab is known as "The City," holds four passengers and is drawn by one horse.

1837: Former Toronto mayor William Lyon Mackenzie leads a failed revolt against British colonial government and the Family Compact. It becomes known as the Upper Canada Rebellion.

1842: Gas service comes to Toronto; water service follows a year later.

1847: The Great Irish Famine brings 38,000 refugees to the city. The population prior to the Irish arrival is 20,000. It creates the greatest civic crisis in the city's history, and the year becomes known as "Black '47."

1849: The Great Fire of 1849 starts early on the morning of Sat., April 7. Much of downtown Toronto is destroyed.

1850: The foundation stone is laid for the Cathedral Church of St. James.

1852: The Toronto Stock Exchange is formed.

1852: St. Michael's College opens in 1852. Marshall McLuhan would later hold the chair of English here until his death in 1980.

1853: The first train to leave Toronto heads north for Barrie on the Toronto, Simcoe and Huron line. Two years later the first east-west train line opens, with the Great Western running between Toronto and Hamilton.

1858: Toronto Island is formed after a severe storm creates a break in the former peninsula.

1861: The first horse-drawn streetcars appear in Toronto, on Yonge Street and Queen Street West.

1867: Confederation gives birth to the Dominion of Canada; Toronto becomes the capital of the new Province of Ontario.

1869: The first dental school in Canada is founded in Toronto. Today it is the Faculty of Dentistry at the University of Toronto.

1869: Timothy Eaton opens his first store, T. Eaton & Co., in Toronto; it begins a national mail-order business in 1884. Simpson's opens in 1872 and goes national in 1885.

1871: The Toronto Trades' Assembly forms, bringing together several unions in one body to lobby for better rights for workers. By the following year 27 unions have joined, including the Cigar Makers' Union, the Bakers' Union and the Typographers' Union.

The Rabble Rouser

Toronto's first mayor, William Lyon Mackenzie, was also Upper Canada's first real firebrand. Born and raised in Scotland by a single mother, he was greatly influenced by her secessionist beliefs. After moving to Canada at age 25, Mackenzie worked on the Lachine Canal, moving to York in 1822 to work for a childhood friend.

There he began writing for the *York Observer*, and when the relationship with his friend cooled, he started his own newspaper, the *Colonial Advocate*. He soon became a person of influence and a well-known and vocal critic of the Family Compact, the elite group of wealthy conservative Anglicans that held formal and informal power in Upper Canada in the first half of the 19th century. What frightened British lawmakers most was Mackenzie's fervent admiration of the emerging democracy of the United States.

Mackenzie's popularity was such that he won his first election to the province's House of Assembly in 1824, and although he was repeatedly expelled, he was repeatedly elected. In 1834, the year York became the City of Toronto, Mackenzie and his reform colleagues won a majority on the first city council.

Mackenzie, however, was more interested in provincial politics (he had kept his seat in the House of Assembly). Deciding not to seek re-election in the city, he instead refocused his efforts at the provincial level. He grew increasingly frustrated, and in 1837 he organized an armed revolt.

The revolt failed but Mackenzie was allowed to escape to the United States, where he was later arrested for breaching neutrality laws after he kept trying to inflame Americans against their northern neighbours. He spent 18 months in jail and 10 years in exile. Many of the changes he demanded – particularly responsible government – were eventually adopted. In many ways, Mackenzie, along with Papineau and Joseph Howe, ushered in the era of democracy in Canada.

Pardoned in 1849, Mackenzie returned to Toronto and was elected to the Assembly of the Province of Canada. He died in Toronto in 1861. His grandson, William Lyon MacKenzie King, would eventually become the longest-serving prime minister in Canadian history.

1874: The first jail for women in Canada, the Andrew Mercer Reformatory, opens on King Street West. It closes in 1969 and is later demolished.

1875: The original Hospital for Sick Children opens.

1877: Emily Stowe organizes the Toronto Women's Literary Club. A few years later it becomes the Toronto Women's Suffrage Club.

Toronto, U.S.A.

The United States' declaration of war against Britain in 1812 meant, by extension, that it was also declaring war against its possessions in the rest of North America, which included York and Upper Canada. The Americans were prompted to the drastic move by their displeasure with British restrictions on trade with France, and by British use of American Indians to impede settlement in the rest of North America.

Although York was the capital of Upper Canada, the British saw the first line of defence against Americans as being Kingston; the fort there had 7,000 men. The fort at York, on the other hand, was manned by just 300 regulars, 400 militia and 50 to 100 Amerindians. So when the Americans landed in York in 1813 with 1,700 highly trained men aboard 14 ships, there was no contest.

British Major-General Robert Hale Sheaffe ordered the fort's surrender, but first he instructed that all military vessels in the harbour be burned and the grand magazine at Fort York detonated. In the ensuing explosion, 38 Americans were killed and another 200 wounded. Today the grand magazine has been rebuilt, and a plaque at Fort York commemorates its destruction.

When the capture of Fort York was complete, the Americans looted and set buildings ablaze, including the Parliament buildings—an act that was repaid in 1814, when the British burned the White House and government buildings in Washington.

1879: The first Canadian National Exhibition (CNE) buildings are built. Construction takes all of 90 days.

1883: Dr. Augusta Stowe graduates from the Toronto School of Medicine; she is the first woman to obtain a degree in medicine in Canada. Previously, female doctors—including Stowe's mother, Emily—were educated in the United States.

1883: The Toronto Electric Light Company is incorporated.

1884: The first free Toronto Public Library opens in the Mechanics' Institute Building at Church and Adelaide.

1884: The Ontario legislature changes voting laws to allow women to vote. Unmarried women and widows owning or renting property assessed at more than $400 are now allowed to participate.

1887: Asphalt roads begin to appear; "Muddy York" begins to disappear.

1894: Massey Hall opens with a performance of Handel's *Messiah*.

1893: William Peyton Hubbard, Toronto's first black politician, is elected alderman for Ward 4, now Trinity-Spadina.

1899: On Sept. 18, City Hall officially opens.

1900: The first tunnel for pedestrians is built under James Street, between Eaton's and the Eaton's Annex.

1904: A fire that starts at 58 Wellington St. on a cold April evening turns into a major conflagration that destroys 100 buildings over 20 acres in the downtown area.

1905: T. Eaton Company sponsors the city's first Santa Claus "parade," transporting Santa from Union Station to the Eaton's store by horse and wagon.

1906: Toronto's first permanent movie theatre, the Theatorium (later called the Red Mill), opens at 183 Yonge St.

TAKE5 KAREN BLACK'S FIVE FAVOURITE
ARTIFACTS IN THE CITY'S HISTORICAL COLLECTION

With more than 100,000 objects dating from the 18th century onward, the City of Toronto has one of the largest civic collections in the country—one that could easily serve a museum focused solely on Canada's largest metropolis. Some are distributed in, or rotated into, the 10 museums the city does run, but the bulk of the collection is in storage. Karen Black is the manager of Museums and Heritage Services for the City of Toronto. "Many of the artifacts in the collection connect personal stories to larger national and international events," she says, "and that's what makes them special." Here is her selection of five gems currently in the vaults.

1. **Heart-shaped box:** Carved by one of the prisoners serving time in the Toronto jail for participating in the 1837 Rebellion. One of the most significant events in Canadian history, the rebellion resulted in responsible government and the democracy we enjoy today. The oak box is inscribed to the prisoner's wife, providing an intimate view of a national story.

2. **Concert button:** The official souvenir button of the Grateful Dead and Jefferson Airplane concert held at the O'Keefe Centre in the summer of love, 1967. The musicians were brought to Toronto for eight nights by legendary American rock-concert promoter Bill Graham.

1909: The Toronto Argonauts play their first game in Varsity Stadium. They will win their first Grey Cup in 1914, beating the University of Toronto.

1911: The first mechanized ambulance service, operated by A.W. Miles Funeral Home, begins operations.

3. **Official 1961 Maple Leaf Gardens program:** For the game between Toronto and Detroit on Nov. 11, 1961. This was one of the seasons when the Leafs won the Stanley Cup. The program is auto-graphed in blue ballpoint pen by several players, including Eddie Shack, Red Kelly, Johnny Bower and Tim Horton.

4. **Jarvis uniform:** One of the oldest garments in the City of Toronto. A captain's uniform of the Queen's Rangers made of green wool, it features a black-velvet collar, cuffs and lapels with embroidered silver lace, epaulettes and metal buttons. It belonged to Colonel William Jarvis, a calvary officer under John Graves Simcoe in the American Revolution. The jacket links the American Revolution with the establishment of Toronto but it also has a personal story; it comes with sweat stains, a tailor's bill and a link to one of Toronto's founding families.

5. **Lady Eaton beaded dress train:** A pink-velvet dress train deco-rated with rhinestones and sequins, with matching fan. It was part of a formal outfit worn by Florence Eaton (1880–1970) on the day in 1915 when she was presented at court in Britain. Her husband, Toronto retail merchant and philanthropist John Craig Eaton (1876–1922), was receiving a knighthood from King George V.

1914: The Toronto General Hospital moves to its new location at the corner of College Street and University Avenue, where it is today.

1921: The Toronto Transportation Commission (later the Toronto Transit Commission, or TTC) is created.

1922: The Boys and Girls House, the first library in the British Empire devoted to children, opens on St. George Street. Banting, Best, Macleod and Collip discover insulin in a University of Toronto laboratory.

1927: Edward, Prince of Wales, opens Union Station on Aug. 6. Conn Smythe buys Toronto's NHL hockey team, the Toronto St. Pats, and renames them the Maple Leafs.

1929: The Royal York Hotel opens on Front Street.

1931: Maple Leaf Gardens opens its doors to hockey fans. Foster Hewitt broadcasts his first game from "the gondola" over centre ice. The Leafs lose 2-1 to Chicago. The Bay and Dundas Gray Coach lines bus station opens.

1932: The Toronto Maple Leafs win their first Stanley Cup, defeating the New York Rangers three straight in a best-of-five series.

1939: Malton Airport (now Lester B. Pearson International) is built.

1947: Cocktail lounges are legalized in the city.

1953: The Province of Ontario creates the Municipality of Metropolitan Toronto, joining the City of Toronto, Etobicoke, North York, Scarborough and York, as well as the smaller communities of East York, Forest Hill, Leaside, Long Branch, Mimico, New Toronto, Swansea and Weston.

The Boy in Blue

Born in 1855 and raised on Toronto Island, Toronto's first sports mega-hero, Ned Hanlan, learned to handle a boat at a young age by rowing across the harbour to meet friends and go to school and by working with his father who fished for a living but later became a hotelier, fuelling the rumour that young Ned also rowed bootleg liquor across for hotel guests.

Hanlan began his rise to prominence by competing successfully in local races. In 1876 he turned professional, winning the Centennial Regatta in Philadelphia. Young and slight compared to his rivals, he typically wore a blue shirt and red headband and soon became known to all who followed his victories as "the boy in blue."

In 1878 and 1880, Hanlan competed in a three-race series with U.S. amateur champion Charles Courtney. It was a huge series in both countries, at a time when rowing was followed as widely as pro sports are today. In the final race in Washington, more than 100,000 people lined the banks of the Potomac River to watch Hanlan stroke to victory.

Through the "challenge" system, Hanlan became Canadian champion in 1877, beating New Brunswick's Wallace Ross on a five-mile course; the American championship in 1878, beating Ephraim Morris on the Allegheny; and English Champion in 1879, beating William Elliott by 11 lengths on the Tyne.

In 1880, Hanlan went head to head on the Thames River against Edward Trickett of Australia, defeating him to become world champion. It is speculated that as much as £100,000 was bet against Hanlan in that race. Always willing to accept a challenge, he would defend his world title six more times in locations around the world before finally losing it to Australian William Beach. The Australians were so impressed with Hanlan's sportsmanship and skill they named a community in New South Wales "Toronto."

Hanlan was widely celebrated as one of the world's greatest oarsman. He was also a pioneer of modern-day sculling technique (he used a sliding seat), and the most popular and well-known athlete in Toronto and the country in the 19th century. When he died in 1908, some 10,000 mourners attended his funeral. In 1926 Hanlan was permanently honoured when the city erected a bronze statue of him on the grounds of Toronto's Canadian National Exhibition.

1954: Toronto's (and Canada's) first subway line opens beneath Yonge Street; trains run between Union and Eglinton stations. Hurricane Hazel devastates the city in October.

1965: Toronto's new City Hall officially opens on Sept. 13.

1966: Ontario creates the Metro level of government, incorporating the cities of Toronto, Etobicoke, North York, Scarborough and York and the borough of East York.

1967: The Toronto Maple Leafs win their 13th Stanley Cup—unlucky 13, as it turns out, because fans are still waiting for No. 14.

1971: The first "Gay Day Picnic" takes place in August at Hanlan's Point.

1976: Toronto's population grows larger than that of Montreal, making it Canada's most populous city. The CN Tower opens.

1977: The Toronto Blue Jays are born. They play their first home game at Exhibition Stadium and beat the Chicago White Sox 9-6 during a minor snowstorm.

1979: Toronto declares February Black History Month; it's the first municipal government in Canada to do so.

1982: Roy Thomson Hall opens on Sept. 13 with a gala concert.

1985: The Scarborough Rapid Transit line opens, expanding subway service to the eastern areas of the city.

1989: The Skydome stadium opens.

1992: The Toronto Blue Jays win their first World Series (they win a second in 1993).

Patrician Toronto

Looking to England—with its Eton, Oxford and Cambridge to mold and shape the military, business and political elite who would carry out the duties of the empire—the aristocratic Torontonians who founded Upper Canada College (UCC) in 1829 designed it to mirror Eton. Their goal was to entrench in Canada an establishment that had the classical education and "proper" values necessary to conduct similar duties here.

And build an establishment it did. Perhaps no other educational institution is as well known both in Toronto and around the country. Although today it offers scholarships to children and young men of lesser means (tuition and board cost $48,000), for most Torontonians and Canadians, UCC remains a place of privilege. Some scholars have suggested that patrician Toronto survived as long as it did because of institutions such as UCC and the network of "old boys" it developed.

The old boys' roll does read like a who's who of the Canadian establishment. Conrad Black famously went here, as did Ken Thomson and his son David, the Eaton family, Ted Rogers, Galen Weston, Harold Ballard and, looking further back, William George Gooderham in 1867, owner of Gooderham Worts Distilleries and president of the Bank of Toronto, among many others. Scholar Jack Granatstein estimates that 20 to 30 percent of the country's generals in the two great wars attended UCC.

Although not the singular force it once was, UCC is still a significant agent in knitting together the future kings of industry. For many Torontonians, especially immigrants, it is partly a mythical place, belonging to another time when the king's sons disappeared to have their rough edges made smooth and their mettle prepared for ruling the realm.

1993: The Toronto Raptors join the NBA.

1997: Seventy-six percent of voters in a referendum oppose the proposed creation of a megacity. It makes little difference. Ontario Premier Mike Harris ignores residents and creates the amalgamated City of Toronto; the new entity becomes effective Jan. 1, 1998.

1998: The amalgamation of the seven library boards into the Toronto Public Library creates the largest public-library system in North America.

1999: The Air Canada Centre opens. The first hockey game, the hometown Maple Leafs, is held on Feb. 20; the first basketball game, the hometown Raptors, is on Feb. 21; and the first concert, The Tragically Hip, is on Feb. 22.

2002: Toronto hosts Pope John Paul II on World Youth Day.

2003: Toronto is hit by the SARS epidemic. Although the disease is primarily confined to hospitals and health care workers, tourism significantly suffers because of media reports. To help recover from the resulting economic losses, the city holds a SARS benefit concert, colloquially named SARSStock, headlined by The Rolling Stones and featuring many other big-name acts, including AC/DC, Rush, The Guess Who and Justin Timberlake.

2003: Toronto goes dark in the Northeast Blackout of 2003. In all, more than 45 million people in Canada and the U.S. fall off the power grid.

2006: The Four Seasons Centre for the Performing Arts, built to host opera and ballet productions, opens at the corner of University Avenue and Queen Street West.

2008: A huge propane blast erupts at the Keele and Wilson neighbourhood of Downsview. Thousands of people are evacuated and two die.

2009: Toronto celebrates its 175th anniversary. The city has the highest foreign-born population of any other urban centre in the world.

Essentials

Location: Canada's largest city spreads along the north shore of Lake Ontario at about the same latitude as the French Riviera. A relatively flat city, Toronto, like most of southern Ontario, sits on a slope of sedimentary rock but is cut by several deep ravines that lead to Lake Ontario. It stretches 43 km east to west, covers 641 sq. km and takes in 138 km of the meandering lakeshore. Its northern border is Steeles Avenue, about 21 km north of the water.

Origin of Name: "Toronto" evolved from the Iroquois word *tkaronto*, or "place where trees stand in water." It was originally applied to the narrow south end of Lake Simcoe, where aboriginal peoples built fishing weirs. In the early 1720s, the French brought the name south along the traditional aboriginal canoe route and gave it to their fort near the mouth of the Humber River. By 1765 Toronto was appearing on English maps. Lieutenant-Governor John Graves Simcoe renamed the young settlement York in 1793, but Toronto was officially re-adopted by popular demand in 1834. Torontonians pronounce the name "Tronno" or "Tuhronna," not "Toe-RON-toe."

Provincial Capital: Toronto began serving as the capital of Upper Canada in 1793 when the previous capital, Newark (now Niagara-on-the-Lake), was considered geographically vulnerable to the new Republic to the south. Governor Simcoe ordered the move to York. Toronto (its first name had by then been restored) became Ontario's capital when Canada was formed in 1867.

Toronto Amalgamation: In 1998, amalgamation merged the former Regional Municipality of Metropolitan Toronto with the former suburb cities of Scarborough, East York, York, North York and Etobicoke. The latter are now known as the "inner suburbs," and the whole "new" city is sometimes referred to as "the megacity."

The GTA: The Greater Toronto Area includes the megacity plus the Region of Durham (including the communities of Oshawa, Whitby, Ajax, Pickering, Brock, Scugog, Uxbridge and Clarington), the Region of Peel (Brampton, Caledon and Mississauga), Halton Region (Burlington, Halton Hills, Oakville and Milton) and York Region (Aurora, East Gwillimbury, Markham, Newmarket, King, Georgina, Richmond Hill, Vaughan and Whitchurch-Stouffville). Collectively they are known by their nicknames, which include "the 905," "the Golden Horseshoe" and the "outer suburbs."

CMA: Toronto CMA (Census Metropolitan Area) refers to the municipalities considered by Statistics Canada "to have a high degree of integration with the City of Toronto, as measured by commuting flows derived from census place of work data." The CMA is slightly smaller than the GTA and comprises the City of Toronto plus 23 other municipalities: Ajax, Aurora, Bradford West Gwillimbury, Brampton, Caledon, East Gwillimbury, Georgina, Georgina Island, Halton Hills, King Township, Markham, Milton, Mississauga, Mono Township, Newmarket, Tecumseth, Oakville, Orangeville, Pickering, Richmond Hill, Uxbridge, Whitchurch-Stouffville and Vaughan.

Nicknames: Muddy York, Hog Town, T.O. (pronounced "tee-oh"), the Big Smoke, Hollywood North, T-dot, the 416, Toronto the Good and the Megacity.

Licence Plate: Torontonians use Ontario licence plates but can buy vanity plates emblazoned with the graphics of the University of Toronto or the Toronto Scottish Regiment, or the logos of the Toronto Blue Jays, Raptors, Maple Leafs and Argonauts.

Motto: "Diversity Our Strength," adopted in 1998 following the creation of the new City of Toronto.

Coat of Arms: Created for the new City of Toronto in 1998, it features a honeycomb, a columbine flower, green grass and three rivers, plus a beaver, a bear and an eagle.

City Flag: Today's city flag is a slight modification of one designed in 1974 by Renato De Santis, then a 21-year-old George Brown College student, for the old City of Toronto. It shows white stylized City Hall office towers on a blue background. A red maple leaf, representing the council chambers, sits at the towers' base.

Incorporation as a City: 1834

Time Zone: Eastern

Area Codes: The Greater Toronto Area is served by seven area codes. The original area code was (416). In 1993 the City of Toronto took over (416) and the GTA was given (905); outer regions such as Durham and York were handed the already in use (705) and Halton and Peel the already in use (519). In 2001 (647) was added to supplement the (416) area code and (289) to supplement the (905) area code. Finally, to supplement the (519) area code, (226) was assigned.

Postal Code Span: M1B to M9W

Statutory Holidays: New Year's Day (Jan. 1), Family Day (third Monday in February), Good Friday (Friday before Easter), Victoria Day (Monday before May 25), Canada Day (July 1), Labour Day (first Monday in September), Thanksgiving (second Monday in October), Christmas Day (Dec. 25) and Boxing Day (Dec. 26).

System of Measurement: Metric

Driving Age: 16

Voting Age: 18

TAKE 5 TRACING THE ROOTS OF FIVE
TORONTO NICKNAMES

1. **Muddy York:** A description of the weather's effect on the unpaved streets old York.
2. **Hogtown:** This is an 1800s' reference to the large volume of live-stock, particularly pigs, processed by Toronto-area abattoirs. A modern play on words, used especially in summer when air pollution hangs over the hot city, is "Smogtown."
3. **The Big Smoke:** Similar to London, England, "the Big Smoke" is a reference to the smog and pollution created by the industrialization of the city in the 19th century. The name is widely believed to have been brought over by British immigrants.
4. **Hollywood North:** Toronto has the third-largest film industry in North America, behind Los Angeles and New York City.
5. **T.O.:** Short for Toronto, Ontario, but recently losing ground to "T-Dot."

TAKE 5 JANE PYPER'S FIVE
ESSENTIAL TORONTO BOOKS

The Toronto Public Library (TPL) is the world's busiest urban public-library system. More than 16 million people visit its 99 branches each year, borrowing more than 29 million items. Its chief librarian, Jane Pyper, has this to say about it: "Our beautiful branches and experienced staff offer safe, welcoming, accessible spaces and services to residents of Toronto, no matter who they are or where they come from." Pyper was part of the management team that merged the city's public libraries following the creation of the megacity. "Toronto is exciting and dynamic, with so much to offer," she says, "just like its library system."

1. *uTOpia: Towards a New Toronto* edited by Alana Wilcox (2005). Featuring passionate visionary essays by 34 journalists, artists, thinkers, architects and activists, uTOpia is a compendium of ideas, opinions and strategies on how to achieve a transformed Toronto.

2. *Historical Atlas of Toronto* by Derek Hayes (2008). Renowned historian Hayes brings Toronto's colourful past to life through stunning maps, rare historical documents and rich stories.

3. *Toronto: No Mean City* by Eric Arthur (1986). First published in 1964, this book sparked the preservation movement of the 1960s and '70s. As Christopher Hume wrote in the 1986 edition, "Arthur's book has become an essential feature on the intellectual landscape of Toronto."

4. *In the Skin of a Lion* by Michael Ondaatje (1987). Ondaatje entwines adventure, romance and history, real and invented, enmeshing us in the lives of the immigrants who built Toronto and those who dreamed it into being.

5. *Cat's Eye* by Margaret Atwood (1988). A painter's return to Toronto triggers reminiscences about the complex and cruel friendships of her youth. Atwood's novel, which provides a vivid picture of Toronto in the 1940s and '50s, shows how dramatically the city had changed by the '80s.

You Know You're From

- Finding a great parking spot can move you to tears.
- You can recommend three reputable body-piercing parlours.
- You think northern Ontario starts at Barrie.
- Despite the 1997 amalgamation, you still use "Scarborough," "Etobicoke" and "North York" in your address.
- When the temperature rises to 5°C you yell, "Woohoo! Patio weather!"
- You haven't been to the CN Tower since you were six but still have nightmares about the turbo elevator.
- You've had at least three bicycles stolen in the past 10 years (you got two of them back when Igor Kenk was arrested).
- You never, ever swim in Lake Ontario.
- You know The Beaches are really called The Beach, but you still say The Beaches to annoy anyone who lives there.
- You've had a birthday party at the Organ Grinder, Spaghetti Factory or The Mad Hatter.
- You couldn't say where Fort York is but you have a vague recollection of having been there in a past life.
- You consider eye contact on the street, subway or streetcar a sign of hostility and an invasion of privacy.
- If it takes you half an hour to get to work by TTC, you are the envy of all your friends.
- You laugh if you hear someone refer to "highway four hundred and one."
- You know that Russell Oliver pays cold hard cash for your used gold and diamonds.
- When you got your first cellphone you thought they were giving you a Barrie number because the area code was 647, not 416.
- They will always be the Skydome, Dundas Square, O'Keefe Centre and Pantages Theatre to you, no matter how many times the names get sold.
- You went clubbing downtown and you were pulled over by a cop on a horse.
- You've been on Speakers' Corner.
- Cito Gaston's return to the Jays made you feel warm and fuzzy.
- You know what the PATH is and can find your way around it.

Toronto When . . .

- You know who can beat Bad Boy furniture's prices: "Noooooobody!"
- You remember looking all over for the "millennium moose"—a painted "art moose" distributed in several locations across the city.
- You live in Little Italy but have Jamaican neighbours on one side and Iranians on the other.
- You gripe about spending 30 minutes on the DVP to get to work but think nothing of spending two hours on the 400 to go to the cottage.
- You eat different ethnic food every night.
- You know the only people talking in an elevator are on their cell-phones.
- You don't know the difference between North Bay and Thunder Bay, but you're pretty sure they're both north of Barrie.
- Everyone you know comes from somewhere else.
- You still think baseball was better when it was played in the snow at Exhibition Stadium.
- You know that to see more than three million people in one place in Toronto you have to go to the Pride Day parade, Caribana or the Santa Claus parade.
- You've been to one of the Rolling Stones' secret concerts.
- You take your kids to High Park or the Toronto Islands so that they can experience nature.
- You believe the Leafs can win the Stanley Cup (and dream you will live to see it).
- You were publicly embarrassed when Mel Lastman called in the army to help with snow removal but privately ecstatic when your street was cleared.
- You only visit the CN Tower, the ROM, the zoo or Casa Loma when you have out-of-town visitors.
- You know the correct answer to "Where do shopping carts go to die?" is "The Don River."
- You know where you were during the 2003 Northeast Blackout.
- You would rather Take The Car than the TTC.
- You leave Toronto and realize how great it is.

Drinking Age: 19

Partnership Cities: Chongqing, China; Chicago, U.S.; Frankfurt, Germany; Milan, Italy.

Friendship Cities: Ho Chi Minh City, Vietnam; Sagamihara, Japan; Quito, Ecuador; Warsaw, Poland; Kiev, Ukraine.

Leafs Nation

The Toronto Maple Leafs are the ongoing soap opera against which all other activities in the city play. Last-place teams, recessions, insane ownership regimes, nine-dollar beer and five-dollar bottles of water have failed to dim demand for tickets that start at $200—and that's if you can get them at all, which of course you often can't. The team defies economic logic, an insolvable problem on which university students write doctoral theses. The Leafs are one of the worst franchises in the league but at the same time the team with the highest valuation.

For members of the Leafs Nation, the past—for the moment, at least—shines with a much brighter light than the future. There is so much to look back upon; the heartbreak is that it was so long ago, the last golden era of Leafs hockey was from 1962–67, when the team captured four Stanley Cups, three of them consecutively. (If you were 10 years old when you saw the Leafs win Lord Stanley's mug in 1967, you are approaching your mid-fifties now.) In 1967 Montreal had won 14 cups to Toronto's 13; today Montreal has captured 24 Stanley Cups.

To give you a measure of exactly how far the Leafs' bar has been lowered, consider the fact that the team's 1992–93 play-off

POPULATION

Toronto is the fifth largest city by population in North America and the 48th largest urban region in the world. Its population of 2,503,285 makes it the largest city in Canada. Toronto has 21.6 percent of the Ontario's 12,160,282 people. A provincial government study predicts the population of Toronto will increase to 3.06 million by 2031, a 16 percent growth rate.

run was the closest sniff since 1967. That year the Leafs took the Gretzky-led Kings to seven games in the semis. That's right, it was the semis, but Doug Gilmour's play during that series has immortalized him forever in the minds of Leafs fans.

For the Leafs Nation, however, there is always a new day, a new owner or general manager that becomes the latest fix. The latest general manager, Brian Burke, has rightly mused publicly that should he be able to hand Leafs fans a Stanley Cup, schools will be named for him. He's right, of course.

It would be a stretch to say there is something mythical about the Leafs, but it would not be out of place to say there is something special. There are large tracts of devout Leafs fans everywhere, from Newfoundland to Vancouver Island. Parents across the country have bequeathed their teams to their children and so on down the line. And the great Leafs diaspora is such that a Leafs game guarantees sell-outs in every rink in the country.

Leafs fans are nothing if not optimistic. They know, like Chicago Cubs fans do, that there will be a day of reckoning. The sun will shine, the Cup will return home and be welcomed like a prodigal son, no questions asked.

TAKE 5 GEOFFREY JAMES' FIVE
TORONTO SPECIAL PLACES

Celebrated photographer Geoffrey James, a Welshman by birth, has been interpreting the city through the camera lens since the 1970s. His book *Toronto* (published 2006 in collaboration with writer Mark Kingwell) celebrates his adopted city in 100 images. "Utopia/Dystopia," a retrospective of his work, was held at the National Gallery of Canada in 2008.

Although I travel frequently, I am not a dutiful tourist. I prefer to stay in one place for some time, and enjoy the daily rhythms of a new world, but not necessarily try to take in all the official sights. Before I moved to Toronto thirteen years ago, I confess to having seen it as less a tourist destination than as a place to do journalistic tasks, including a couple of commissions to photograph the city. When I settled here, I decided to photograph Toronto for myself, in an effort to learn about it, and to come to terms with its sometimes elusive civic personality.

Three years of photographing resulted in a book that I like to think of as a portrait of a friend who is not perfect. My list of what to photograph avoids the usual Chamber of Commerce things – the easily-branded engines of tourism, such as our recently refurbished museums, or the CN Tower, which exists in a space that perfectly reflects the sociopathic tendencies of large corporations. What follows are peculiarly, and wonderfully, Toronto places.

1. **Ward's Island** is a short ferry ride from Toronto's strangely bland waterfront, a funky collection of cottages – homesteads really – nestled among the trees. Being there is like going back to the Sixties, and on a summer evening the city across the water glows magically and emits an electrifying basso profundo hum.

2. **The University of Toronto St. George Campus** has many virtues – including doing no harm on its fringes the way many campuses do with fast-food outlets and ratty frat houses. It has a great variety of spaces and buildings, and in recent years has become an exemplary

anthology of contemporary architecture. My favourite is Diamond & Schmitt's Bahen Centre for Information Technology on St. George Street, which artfully hides its considerable bulk behind a façade that wraps around one of the city's handsome yellow-brick houses. It is one of those rare modern buildings that successfully uses decoration, and its southern façade, when viewed from College Street, is as satisfying as something by Borromini.

3. **The Bain Housing Co-Op**, which stretches out on both sides of a Sycamore-lined street of the same name in the east end, was built in 1914 and is Toronto's first experiment with social housing. The houses open onto courtyards, and in the summer the back lanes are a riot of vegetation. In a city that often welcomes you with folded arms, the mood here is always friendly. It is the closest thing to Utopia that I have found in Toronto.

4. Further east, the **R.C. Harris Water Purification Plant**, between Queen Street and Lake Ontario, is Toronto's greatest public work, a fabulous '30s Art Deco palace that was built to last. Michael Ondaatje mythologized both it and its maker in *The Skin of the Lion*. It is currently being modified, but remains a reminder of the pleasures of anything done very well. Canadians, as the poet and lawyer Frank Scott once said, tend never to do anything by halves that they can do by quarters.

5. I must confess to never having gone inside the **Spadina Museum**, the home that William Warren Baldwin built in early 19th century outside and above the Town of York. Nowadays the house is next to the absurd millionaire pile known as Casa Loma, and on the edge of prosperous Forest Hill. I go for the grounds – wonderful chestnut and maple trees, a fabulous kitchen garden and orchard. It is good in every season, and whenever I feel the need to photograph a tree, I head up the hill to Mr. Baldwin's mansion.

POPULATION IN PERSPECTIVE

Toronto	2,503,285
Montreal	1,620,693
Vancouver	1,986,965
Calgary	988,193
Ottawa	812,129

Source: Statistics Canada

TAKE 5 JOHN ROBERT COLOMBO'S TOP FIVE QUIPS AND QUOTES ABOUT TORONTO

John Robert Colombo is known as "the master gatherer" for his compilations of Canadiana. A long-time resident of North York in Toronto, he has written, compiled or translated 200 books, including *The Toronto Puzzle Book* and *Haunted Toronto*.

1. *"Toronto is a clean idea between two dirty rivers."*
— **Harold Town, artist (1960)**

2. *"If you're born in a city like London or Paris, you know you were born to one of the oldest cultures in the world. If you're born in a city like New York, you know you were born to be one of the kings of the world. But if you're born in Toronto—that's destiny."*
— **Moses Znaimer, media personality (1984)**

3. *"Toronto is a kind of New York operated by the Swiss."*
— **Peter Ustinov, theatre personality (1987)**

4. *"Cheer up! You have drawn a second prize, I would say, in the Lottario of Life."*
— **Jan Morris, travel writer (1990)**

5. *"Even though it's lost its raison d'étre, it's still incredibly comfortable."*
— **Tyler Brûlé, editor and socialite (2008)**

TAKE*5* TOP FIVE VISIBLE MINORITY
GROUPS IN TORONTO

1. **South Asian:** 12 percent
2. **Chinese:** 11.4 percent
3. **Black:** 8.4 percent
4. **Filipino:** 4.1 percent
5. **Latin American:** 2.6 percent

Source: Statistics Canada and City of Toronto

POPULATION DENSITY (PEOPLE/SQ. KM)

Montreal	4,438.7
Toronto	**3,972.4**
Edmonton	1,067.2
New York City	10,194.2
Ontario	22.3
Canada	3.3

IMMIGRATION/DEMOGRAPHIC CHANGE

Between 2001 and 2006, more than a quarter of a million (267,855) new immigrants moved to Toronto. In 2005 alone, 58,255 new immigrants arrived and the city grew a further 11,020, as people moved to Toronto from another Canadian province or territory.

BOYS AND GIRLS

Age	Male	Female	Total
0–14	210,505	199,115	409,620
15–64	845,305	894,900	1,740,205
65+	149,560	203,885	353,445

Did you know...

that almost half of the people living in Toronto were not yet born when the Maple Leafs last won the Stanley Cup?

TAKE 5 TORONTO'S TOP FIVE MOTHER
TONGUE LANGUAGES OTHER THAN ENGLISH

1. **Chinese**
2. **Italian**
3. **Punjabi**
4. **Spanish**
5. **Portuguese**

Source: Statistics Canada

POPULATION BY AGE

In 2006, 83.6 percent of Torontonians were older than 15, slightly higher than the average for the province (81.8 percent). The median age in the city was 38.4, just under Ontario's median age of 39.

MEDIAN AGE

- Men: 37.4
- Women: 39.3

LIFE EXPECTANCY

Men	Ontario: 75	Canada: 77.7
Women	Ontario: 81	Canada: 82.5
Fertility rate	Ontario: 1.5	Canada: 1.5

Did you know...

that Henrietta Lane near Church and Front streets was the hub of prostitution in the early 1800s? The brothels were close to the harbour, convenient for anyone travelling to or from York.

They said it

"It may be a cliché to say that Toronto is a city of neighbour-hoods, but it is one of very few great world cities that really does still have neighbourhoods, where people of different classes and ethnicities can mix and mingle, and where neighbourhood shopping districts are not overwhelmed by chains."

– Richard Florida, in *Toronto: A City Becoming*

CRADLE TO GRAVE

Births (yearly 2007-08)   Ontario: 136,217   Canada: 364,085
Birth rate Toronto: 11.5   Ontario: 10.6   Canada: 10.5
Deaths (yearly 2007-08)   Ontario: 88,680   Canada: 237,202
Death rate Toronto: 5.5   Ontario: 7.1   Canada: 7.3

ON A TYPICAL DAY IN TORONTO . . .

- 82 babies are born
- 49 people die

FAMILY STRUCTURE

- Percentage of families that are married couples: 69
- Common-law families: 9
- Female lone-parent families: 19
- Male lone-parent families: 3
- Average number of people per family: 3

Source: Statistics Canada

Did you know. . .

that Toronto is ranked No. 1 in North America for Best Quality of Life and Top City Region of the Future by *FDI Magazine*, and ranked second in North America and 15th worldwide in the 2008 Mercer Human Resources Quality of Living survey?

They said it

RELIGIOUS AFFILIATION (PERCENTAGE)

Catholic: 31.4

Protestant: 21.2

Other Christian: 3.9

Christian Orthodox: 4.9

Buddhist: 2.7

Muslim: 6.7

Hindu: 4.9

Jewish: 4.2

Eastern religions: 0.2

Sikh: 0.9

Other religions: 0.1

None: 18.9

Source: Statistics Canada.

LANGUAGE (PERCENTAGE)

- English only: 64.4
- French only: 0.5
- Non-official language: 31.1

Source: Statistics Canada

STUDENTS ENROLLED

Universities: 147,676

Colleges (provincial): 218,753

PUBLIC SCHOOLS
- Toronto District School Board: 284,000 (includes adults)
- Toronto Catholic District School Board: 91,675
- Conseil scolaire de district du Centre-Sud-Ouest (French Public Board): 2,524
- Conseil scolaire de district catholique Centre-Sud (French Catholic): 1,800

HEALTH CARE PROFESSIONALS
Physicians – 7,325
Pharmacists – 3,565 **
Dentists – 2,296
Nurses – 18,254 ***

** includes Mississauga

*** includes 15,612 registered nurses, 2,562 registered practical nurses and 80 nurse practitioners. These statistics are for Toronto Central Local Health Integration Network (LHIN) only.

CANADIAN COMMUNITY HEALTH SURVEY
(Percentage of respondents who…)

	Toronto	Ontario	Canada
Are overweight	29.5	33.3	33.3
Are physically active	44.1	50	50.4
See a doctor regularly	82	81.1	80
Smoke regularly	19.7	22.1	22.9

Source: Canadian Community Health Survey

Did you know...

that you can find seven cities called Toronto in the U.S. and one in Australia?

COMMUNICATIONS

Daily: *Toronto Star, Toronto Sun, The Globe and Mail, National Post, Metro, 24*

Weekly: *Now, Eye, The Epoch Times*, and nine weekly neighbourhood-based Metroland papers; *Xtra* and *FAB* magazines (for the gay, lesbian, bisexual and trans-gendered community)

Ethnic: 79 ethnic newspapers/magazines, including *Share* (Canada's largest ethnic newspaper) and *Sing Tao* (a Chinese-language daily newspaper)

Business: Approximately 400 business periodicals

TV/cable broadcasting source stations: Close to a dozen TV stations

AM/FM radio stations: Just under 30

Weblinks

City of Toronto

www.toronto.ca

This website has lots of useful information for both residents and visitors, including history, news, local services, cultural and other events and political happenings.

Toronto.com Be in the Know

www.toronto.com

Owned by the *Toronto Star*, this website provides information about entertainment, dining, events, movies and more. It also has great contests.

blogTO

www.blogto.com

A comprehensive blog, part of the Fresh Daily Network, that updates readers on happenings in the city's political, cultural and community arenas.

Slang

Torontonians refer to many of the city's sayings, fixtures, landmarks and byways in a kind of short form that can be impenetrable to newcomers. Here's a primer.

ACC: The Air Canada Centre is the new incarnation of Toronto's former Canada Post Delivery Building. It has been hosting NHL, NBA and NLL sports teams and concert performers since it opened in 1999.

AGO: The Art Gallery of Ontario has more than 68,000 works by artists from around the globe in its collection.

Arrrr-goooooooos!: Chant heard at Toronto Argonaut football games and in downtown streets long after the game is over.

Asian Court: The Agincourt area of Scarborough. After an influx of Hong Kong Chinese and Taiwanese and the development of Agincourt's Dragon Centre Mall in the 1980s, it became a booming Chinatown and was the vanguard for the proliferation of Chinese malls—large malls with restaurants and stores catering specifically to the Chinese community.

Bring in the Army: Mayor Mel (former mayor Mel Lastman) called upon Canada's Armed Forces to help with snow removal after a series of major snowfalls in January of 1999. Since then, any significant snowfall might generate quips that it's time to "bring in the army."

The Buds: Affectionate name for the Toronto Maple Leafs, the city's agony and ecstasy. Known to disgruntled or rival hockey fans as the Make Me Laughs or the Make Believes.

Crappy Tire: Elsewhere in Canada, the Canadian Tire Corp. is a respected institution. In the Greater Toronto Area, or the GTA, not so much.

Don Valley Parking Lot: The Don Valley Parkway, the city's busiest north-south thoroughfare, slows to a crawl during rush hour. Commonly called the DVP.

The Ex: The Canadian National Exhibition, also known as the CNE. For 18 days leading up to Labour Day more than a million visitors click through the CNE gates to view the special exhibits, ride the roller coasters and play midway games where the skilled and lucky may win a Stewie Griffin kewpie doll. The Ex is all about noise, nostalgia, old-fashioned fun and retro food. (Tip: A styrofoam bowl of spaghetti covered with bottled pasta sauce can be bought for 99 cents, then search out the cool doughnut-maker machine for dessert.)

Eg-ling-ton: Try to find five Torontonians who pronounce Eglinton Avenue, uptown Toronto's main east-west street, the way it is spelled: with only one G sound. Eglinton is sometimes shortened to Egg, as in "the intersection of Yonge and Egg."

FOB: Fresh off the boat. Chinese use this more than Anglophones to contrast with CBC, or Chinese-born Canadian.

Gardiner: Refers to the Gardiner Expressway, named for first chairman of the Metro level of government, Frederick Golden "Big Daddy" Gardiner.

Gaybourhood: The Church and Wellesley area, just east of Yonge Street, has numerous bars, restaurants and stores serving the local gay community and is home to the annual Gay Pride Parade celebration, one of the largest in North America. It's dubbed "The Village" by locals and also called the "Gay Village" and the "Gay Ghetto."

Gina: A female, usually of Mediterranean descent, who dresses in tight clothing and uses excessive amounts of hair products.

TAKE 5 PIER GIORGIO DI CICCO'S FIVE
WAYS TO DESCRIBE TORONTO

Pier Giorgio Di Cicco, Toronto's second poet laureate, was appointed in 2004. An ordained Catholic priest, he is the author of 20 volumes of poetry as well as an urban consultant, curator of the Toronto Museum Project and the recipient of a 2007 Canadian Urban Institute Urban Leadership Award. "Toronto can be defined as a city of no left turns; this exemplifies her age-old ability to say no instead of yes and to love protocol instead of imagination," he says. "That is changing, thanks to new Canadians and young people; she was a 'no' town, becoming a 'maybe' town, trying to become a 'yes' town."

1. **Toronto is circumspect.** She has a history of loyalists and Methodists and Hudson's Bay accountants. So she fares better in a recession.

2. **Toronto is patient.** She waits for her citizens to become affectionate about her.

3. **Toronto is a haven for those who have come with an emotional deficit.** She negotiates space carefully for her children but secretly yearns to be carefree.

4. **Toronto is eager to wear some makeup.**

5. **Toronto is the Emerald City**, still fighting the Wicked Witch of the West, who rides her broom of political correctness. It is the place everyone wants to emigrate to.

Gino: A male, usually of Mediterranean descent, who dresses in tight clothing, wears gold chains, listens to European techno music known as "gino beats" and exhibits a macho attitude. Ginas are usually labelled as a result of their association with ginos.

GO: The brand name for the inter-regional train and bus system that links Toronto with the GTA (pronounced "Go").

Jump Up: A participant in the city's wildly colourful and energetic Caribana parade held each August is said to "jump up." Caribana is North America's largest Caribbean festival and blazes with the excitement of calypso, steel-pan drums and elaborate masquerade costumes.

LRT: Light Rail Transit, the new infrastructure extending the reach of existing subway lines.

Mangia-checche: Pronounced "manja-cake" and loosely meaning "cake-eater," used by Italian immigrants to describe the anglophones they encountered. Probably begun as a criticism of the dominant culture's bland culinary habits, it's now applied more generally as a humorous cultural critique. Sometimes abbreviated to "caker."

TAKE 5 FIVE PHRASES THAT WILL MAKE YOU SOUND LIKE A LOCAL

1. **I never go north of Bloor:** This is used by ultra-urbanites who consider "north of Bloor" to be the boonies.
2. **The Five Thieves:** An affectionate term for a group of five specialty food purveyors in the upscale Summerhill area who charge eyebrow-raising prices.
3. **Four-sixteen:** The original Toronto area code, sometimes used interchangeably by younger Torontonians for the city's name.
4. **How zit go-an?:** A friendly and familiar greeting. Must be articulated precisely.
5. **Young and Eligible:** An area bounded by Yonge and Eglinton where many young urban professionals reside.

TAKE 5 DESMOND COLE'S FIVE TAKES
ON T.O. URBAN SLANG

Desmond Cole won Toronto's 2006 City Idol contest, which was a Canadian Idol-type of event to attract new candidates to civic politics. He chose to run in Trinity–Spadina (the riding recently held by Olivia Chow, who has since moved to Ottawa as an MP) but lost to Adam Vaughan. Cole grew up in Toronto but his parents are from Sierra Leone. "Like so many people, I came to Toronto with big dreams and a little pocket change," he says. "Every day in this city is an adventure and a challenge, but I know how lucky I am to call Toronto my home." He's currently coordinating I Vote Toronto, a campaign to extend municipal-voting rights to immigrants in the city.

1. **Mustang Salad:** Garden produce fertilized with horse feces that has been lifted from a city street, sidewalk or bicycle lane. Local agitators have been known to express solidarity and irony by hurling the produce (of the gardens, not the horses) at mounted riot police.

2. **Line Dancing:** The practice of repeatedly peering down a subway tunnel or track in the belief that such an action will hasten transit. Line dancing is more likely to hasten a close shave by an oncoming train.

3. **Plan-handler:** Any individual who is paid to beg on the sidewalk on behalf of a hospital, charity or children's wilderness group. These benign smiling folks differ from panhandlers in that they offer convenient monthly payment plans and need not fear confrontation from passing police officers.

4. **Layaway:** The act of lying across three seated passengers in the back seat of a taxi to avoid having to pay for two taxis en route to a bar or club. The lone individual in the front seat is thus the only person who can access his or her wallet, leading to increased savings.

5. **New Year's "Hey":** The act of greeting complete strangers as one stumbles home from New Year's Eve festivities. With the possible exception of Halloween, Torontonians can only tolerate such public warmth while drunk and disoriented. The pleasantries are not to be repeated during the following 364 days.

May 2-4 Weekend: During the Victoria Day long weekend in May, partiers pick up a twofer or two-four (a case of 24 beer) and celebrate the Queen's birthday. This holiday is also known by locals as Fireworks Day because of the many pyrotechnical displays seen along the harbourfront and in backyards throughout the GTA.

PATH: A 27-km underground walkway with more than one thousand shopping, service and entertainment venues. In its logo, each letter is a different colour and represents a cardinal direction: P (red) for south, A (orange) for west, T (blue) for north, H (yellow) for east.

QEW: The Queen Elizabeth Way, also known as the Q, the QE and the Queen E. It's the 400-series freeway linking Toronto with the Niagara Peninsula and Buffalo, New York.

Red Rocket: A term of endearment for a type of streetcar introduced by the Toronto Transit Commission in 1938 and which still runs for special charters. Today some people still refer to taking the TTC as "riding the Red Rocket."

TAKE 5 STREET SPEAK

Shorthand for some famous streets and corners.

1. **Yonge and Egg:** The intersection of Yonge and Eglinton.

2. **Roncie:** Roncesvalles Avenue has been the hub of Toronto's Polish community since the 1950s. The south end of this street, where King meets Queen and both meet Roncie, is a major transit terminus.

3. **Vic Park:** Victoria Park Avenue.

4. **Av and Dav:** The intersection of Avenue and Davenport roads.

5. **The Danny:** Danforth Avenue, the key east-end strip that runs from the Bloor Street Viaduct through Greektown to Scarborough.

ROM: Located in the heart of the city, the Royal Ontario Museum contains collections in the earth and life sciences, archaeology and the decorative arts. Pronounced "romm."

Scarberia: Downtowners are notoriously hard on their suburban cousins. For many of them, northern Ontario begins at Highway 401 or "north of Steeles" (Steeles Avenue). But their favourite target is Scarborough, the city's easternmost borough, population 598,000. Ethnically diverse and the greenest part of the GTA, it has a long history and many beautiful features, including the Scarborough Bluffs. "Scarbara" residents have developed their own unique sense of humour, as evidenced by comedian Mike Myers, whose *Wayne's World* character was inspired by growing up there.

Short-turning: An obnoxious habit of Toronto's transit buses and streetcars. It is signalled by the driver blandly announcing, "This streetcar will be short-turning at Spadina Avenue [or wherever]. All passengers must disembark at the next stop."

Special Tea: After-hours beer served in teapots in certain Chinatown restaurants.

TTC: The Toronto Transit Commission is the backbone of the city but also the brunt of jokesters and ranters because of the common experiences Torontonians have had while "riding the Red Rocket."

The Bitter Way: One of the numerous takes on the TTC slogan "The Better Way."

TIFF: The Toronto International Film Festival, which is held every September and pronounced "tiff."

Vomit Comet: After midnight, TTC buses hurl along Bloor and Yonge Streets to replace the subways that have shut down. Inside, some passengers—especially on Friday and Saturday nights—have been known to do the same.

People

Like the waves that wash upon its shoreline, different ethnic groups have swept into Toronto and put their stamp on the land. For millennia, several First Nations tribes inhabited the area around Lake Ontario, either permanently or as a temporary location for trading, hunting and fishing. Then came the French and, later, the English, reflecting the ups and downs of the battle for a continent. They were followed by Americans, free blacks and blacks from the underground railroad. In 1847 more than 38,000 Irish overwhelmed a city of 20,000.

Asian immigration ebbed and flowed throughout the city's more recent history, slowed at times by racist federal immigration policy and laws of exclusion. A resurgence of immigration from Asia in the latter part of the 20th century has had a profound influence. When displaced Hong Kong residents sought to escape China's takeover by moving to Toronto (and elsewhere in Canada), these Chinese became a major force and one of the largest ethnic groups in the city.

Toronto has benefited from its many waves of immigration. Early in the 20th century, Germans made their mark here. After World War II they were joined by others, notably Italians, Greeks, Indians, Vietnamese, Filipinos, Koreans, Africans, West Indians and South Americans. Together they have made Toronto the city in North America with the highest number of foreign-born citizens.

Up until the last 25 years, the establishment attempted to hold to its patrician English roots, but those efforts have largely been swept away. Today Toronto embraces its ethnic diversity, and shop and restaurant signs written in many languages dot the cityscape.

City government has taken to using diversity to attract business. There is also increasing interaction between different ethnic communities. For example, 6.1 percent of married or common-law couples in Toronto are interracial, almost double the Canadian average. It is this broad ethnic and cultural diversity that prompted *National Geographic* to call Toronto "the most civil and civilized city in the world."

FOREIGN-BORN POPULATION

Toronto	45.7 percent
Vancouver	39.6 percent
Montreal	32.9 percent
Calgary	25.9 percent
Winnipeg	19.6 percent
Halifax	8 percent

Source: Statistics Canada

IMMIGRANTS AS A SHARE OF TOTAL POPULATION

Canada	18 percent
United States	10 percent
Germany	9 percent
France	6 percent
Sweden	5 percent
United Kingdom	4 percent
Ireland	3 percent
Finland	2 percent

Source: Toronto Financial Services Alliance

They said it

"Toronto has defined itself not by drawing lines but by erasing them. Every time this city gets into trouble, makes a mistake, does something it lives to regret, it's because it has forgotten the true idea of itself as an idea of inclusion."

– John Ralston Saul

IMMIGRANT POPULATION GROWTH

Between 2001 and 2006, some 1,109,980 immigrants arrived in Canada from other countries, and about one-quarter of them— 267,855, or 55,000 annually—ended up in Toronto. During the same period, the visible minority population increased by 10.6 percent (a 31.8 percent increase since 1996).

Source: City of Toronto

WELCOME TO THE NEIGHBOURHOOD

Toronto suburbs have experienced growing immigrant populations in recent years. The top five are:

- Markham: 65.4 percent
- Brampton: 57 percent
- Mississauga: 49 percent
- Richmond Hill: 45.7 percent
- Ajax: 35. 6 percent

Source: City of Toronto

Did you know...

that in 1989, the United Nations named Toronto the world's most multicultural city?

VISIBLE MINORITIES

As of 2006, 46.9 percent of the residents of Toronto proper belonged to a visible-minority group. This number is expected to continue to grow, and visible minorities are projected to comprise the major population group in Toronto by 2017. The top five visible minority groups are:

- South Asian: 298,372 or 12 percent
- Chinese: 283,075 or 11.4 percent
- Black: 208,555 or 8.4 percent
- Filipino: 102,555 or 4.1 percent
- Latin American: 64,860 or 2.6 percent

Source: City of Toronto

TAKE5 FIVE MAJOR TORONTO
ETHNIC/CULTURAL CELEBRATIONS

1. **Caribana:** This two-week festival on the lakeshore, now in its third decade, is the largest Caribbean festival in North America. A parade, outdoor concerts and band competitions showcase a wide range of indigenous songs, instrumental music, dances, masquerade and oral traditions. The festival introduced Toronto to Caribbean foods and folkways.

2. **Toronto Jewish Film Festival:** Well into its second decade, TJFF presents features, shorts and documentaries on Jewish culture and heritage and is the largest Jewish film festival in North America.

3. **Krinos Taste of the Danforth:** A feast of Hellenic food, culture, and music—from souvlaki to mezes and authentic Greek music to interactive children's games—along the Greek section of Danforth Avenue.

4. **Toronto Dragon Boat Festival:** Founded by the Toronto Chinese Business Association in 1989, the festival is built around the Dragon Boat race, now an international competition, which in turn is based on an ancient Chinese tradition. More than 180 teams compete annually.

5. **Toronto Pride Festival:** One of the largest of its kind in the world, Pride is a three-day arts fest celebrating diverse sexual and gender identities, histories, cultures, creativities, families, friends and lives.

SHARING INFORMATION

Immigration is mainly a federal responsibility, but because Toronto is the major Canadian destination for immigrants, the city provides many services for its newest citizens, including those related to employment, housing and social programs. Dialling 211 gets you free and confidential information available in 15 languages. The city's interpreter service can help out in more than 100 languages.

Newcomers can learn about Toronto's people and culture through daily newspapers published in a variety of languages, including Korean, Italian, Chinese and Spanish. The Toronto Transit Commission (TTC) offers print (and soon online) information on routes and schedules in more than 70 different languages, including Chinese, French, Greek, Italian, Korean, Polish, Portuguese, Russian, Spanish, Tamil, Turkish and Vietnamese.

MEDIAN INCOME BY PERIOD OF IMMIGRATION

Before 1961	$23,070
1961-1970	$29,538
1971-1980	$30,248
1981-1990	$23,639
1991-1995	$18,743
1996-2001	$14,003

Immigrant population's average earnings over that period: $22,595
Non-immigrant population's average earnings over the same period: $30,106

Source: City of Toronto

Did you know. . .

that Toronto has one of the largest Italian communities outside Italy, the largest Portuguese community in North America and the largest Chinese community in Canada?

THE FIRST PEOPLE

Toronto's original settlers were the First Nations peoples. When French traders first arrived, the area was a Seneca (Iroquois) domain. In the early 18th century, when Ojibwa tribes began to move into southern Ontario, the Ojibwa Mississauga Indians replaced the Iroquois along the north shore of Lake Ontario. Their most important village was located in what is now called Baby Point in Toronto's west end.

TAKE 5 DR. JOSEPH WONG'S FIVE
MEMORIES OF ARRIVING IN TORONTO

Born in Hong Kong in 1948, Joseph Wong came to Canada at age 19. He earned a degree in electrical engineering from McGill and a medical degree from the Albert Einstein College of Medicine in New York City before moving to Toronto for post-doctoral work. Dr. Wong has kept up an incredible pace of work and volunteering ever since. A leader in the fight against racism and discrimination in the media and the workplace, he has inspired legions of Torontonians. In 1987 he spearheaded the dream of 30 friends to create the Yee Hong Centre for Geriatric Care; today four centres in the GTA serve four to five thousand seniors. Yee Hong has become the largest non-profit geriatric centre in the country and delivers cultural and language-appropriate services to seniors of Chinese, South-Asian, Filipino and Japanese descent, among others.

1. **On "weekend":** I graduated from an English-grammar high school in Hong Kong, with a good range of English vocabulary. When I first came to Canada, I was scratching my head: What is "weekend"? In Hong Kong in the 1950s, my father, like a lot of other people in the neighbourhood, worked seven days a week to make ends meet. "Weekend" was a strange word to me; it never existed before I came to Canada.

2. **On "downtown":** Another strange word to me at that time. Hong Kong was, and still is, a place where everywhere is dazzling and

Today Toronto is home to about 40,000 native peoples and a large number of Métis. The Ojibwa and members of the Iroquois Six Nations Confederacy are the largest groups in the city's First Nations community. One-third of Ontario's Indian territories are within 320 km of Toronto, and the native community has grown significantly over the last three decades as people have left the provincial territories for jobs in the city.

buzzing, and it is difficult to find a place without huge neon lights and business activities. It is almost impossible to find a place that is not "downtown."

3. **On "diversity" and "multiculturalism":** When there are over 150 languages spoken in Toronto schools, and over half of the population is born outside of the country, "diversity" takes on a new dimension. Everybody feels "at home." One might expect huge problems among so many different cultures and languages, such a non-homogeneous state. Toronto has something to be proud of: harmony.

4. **On "immigrant" and "newcomer":** It was a conscious decision to choose Canada as my home. For the first five years I was in Canada, I never changed the time on my watch: it was always on Hong Kong time. On the day I got married in 1973, and I decided this country was going to be my permanent home, my watch reflected the change of my mind and heart.

5. **On "going home":** Like other immigrants, I believed "going home" in the first few years meant going back to where I came from. Now, many Chinese seniors have been in Canada for a decade or more, so going home means coming back to Toronto, where there are all the amenities they need, the clean air they enjoy, and yes, the blue sky and the white clouds.

IRISH

During the summer of 1847, roughly 38,000 Irish fleeing the Great Potato Famine arrived at Toronto harbour; the city itself had a population of a mere 20,000. More than 1,100 immigrants died of typhus in "fever sheds" built on the wharves where the ships docked.

Most Irish Catholics settled east of Yonge Street in a slum area

The Ward

The glittering block of high-rise office towers, hotels and condos bounded by Yonge, College, University and Queen was once a gateway slum for the city's most persecuted and penniless immigrants. Officially named St. John's Ward and one of the city's municipal units, it was from the 1850s to the 1950s simply known as the Ward.

The Ward was a warren of narrow lanes packed with ramshackle hovels and dingy storefronts. Muddy alleys were cluttered with garbage and clothes hanging to dry. The air stunk of rot and waste. Conditions were equally crowded and squalid indoors. In 1913 the Department of Health reported that at least 3,000 houses in the Ward were being occupied by two to six families.

While most Ward residents were hard-working and law abiding, the stigma of vice and criminality hung over the slum. The neighbourhood was rife with bootleggers, gambling dens and brothels. The immigrants who lived there were subject to heavy-handed police action in the enforcement of morality laws.

The Ward shrank over the 20th century, most notably in 1909 when eight acres of housing were demolished to make way for the construction of the Toronto General Hospital, and again when streets were widened to allow the downtown commercial district to grow. The deathblow came with the expropriation of much of the Ward for the site of the new City Hall and Nathan Phillips Square in the late 1950s. The Ward has now been entirely erased from the cityscape and, for the most part, from the memory of Toronto citizens.

They said it

called Corktown, south of Queen Street, or mingled with other immigrants along Parliament Street in what became known as Cabbagetown. Some also moved into a ramshackle settlement known as the Ward.

Irish Protestants were welcomed into British society. By the 1920s, Toronto was called "The Belfast of Canada," and Orangemen parades took four hours to pass a given point. The dour Victorian values represented by the Orange Order lasted far longer in "Toronto the Good" than they had in Britain, prompting painter Wyndham Lewis to call the city "a sanctimonious icebox" in the 1940s.

As a consequence, Irish Catholics experienced severe intolerance and discrimination. This harsh treatment caused many violent incidents that culminated in the Jubilee Riots of 1875, when a pilgrimage of Catholic worshippers was repeatedly attacked by stone-throwing mobs. Over time, Irish Catholic initiatives, such as the founding of St. Michael's College (1852), three hospitals, and the most significant charitable organizations in the city, strengthened the Irish identity, gradually transforming their presence into one of influence and power.

In 2007 a famine memorial was erected in Ireland Park at the foot of Bathurst Street to remember those who had died in the fever sheds. Four life-size bronze figures depict the Irish in all of their misery, and the names of 600 of the deceased have been carved into a wall.

JEWS

The growth of the Jewish community has always depended on waves of immigration caused by persecution. Between 1911 and 1921, anti-Jewish pogroms in Eastern Europe caused Toronto's Jewish population to nearly double to 34,619. Jews settled principally in the Ward, an overcrowded neighbourhood filled with shops and close to many sweatshops that employed Jewish labourers. During the 1920s, they

Bio Olivia Chow

In 1970 Olivia Chow, who was then 13, immigrated to Toronto with her family from Hong Kong. In 1991 she became the first Asian woman to be voted onto Toronto's city council, and she's now one of the best-known immigrant women in the country.

Recognized as both an environmental and social-justice advocate, Chow was a city councillor who practiced what she preached. While on council she rode her bike to work in all kinds of weather, in part to model ways of saving energy. After many of her bicycles were stolen, she decorated one with plastic flowers figuring no self-respecting thief would steal it. The flowered bike became her trademark.

As the city's first children and youth advocate, Chow spearheaded efforts such as free dental care for poor children and expanded pre- and post-natal services. She also led the charge to create a children's nutrition program that within a few years was feeding more than 70,000 children.

Following a number of high-profile cases of police misconduct, Chow sought an appointment to the Police Services Board. Ever combative, she was forced to resign her post after urging police to change their tactics during a riot in front of the legislature building.

In 2006 Chow was elected to represent Trinity-Spadina for the NDP on her third attempt at winning the federal seat. In Ottawa she joined NDP leader Jack Layton as part of only the second husband-and-wife team in Canadian parliamentary history.

moved westward and established the Jewish Market, now Kensington Market, where 80 percent of Jews were living at that time.

By 1931 Jews represented the largest non-British minority in Toronto and became the target of xenophobic prejudice. Discriminatory federal laws stopped further immigration and struck a terrible blow to European Jews trying to escape Nazism. In 1933 a six-hour riot broke out during a baseball game at Christie Pits, when young men belonging to the Swastika Club displayed their hateful symbol painted in black on a white bed sheet.

After World War II, further large waves of Jewish immigration occurred, and then again when Quebec separatism spurred many to leave Montreal. By 1960 the community had left Kensington Market and moved to North York and beyond, taking with them numerous bookstores, kosher markets and delis. Today Toronto is home to 164,000 Jews and nearly 60 synagogues serving every branch of Judaism.

TAKE 5 FIVE NON-ENGLISH RADIO STATIONS IN TORONTO

1. **CHIN:** Broadcasts out of Toronto and Ottawa in more than 30 languages, reaching a broad swath of people across southern Ontario. (AM 1540, FM 100)

2. **CKWR:** An independent non-profit community radio station with news and programming in 22 languages, including German, Portuguese, Polish, Romanian, Spanish, Greek, Croatian and Italian. (FM 98.5)

3. **CMR:** North America's only South Asian-owned-and-operated radio station, Canadian Multicultural Radio represents a growing ethnic voice in the GTA, servicing 20 ethnic groups in more than 24 languages. (101.3 FM)

4. **CIRV:** Predominantly Portuguese, CIRV transmits in 12 languages, uniting listeners with common backgrounds, goals and interests. (88.9 FM)

5. **Punjabi Lehran:** Offers talk shows, daily news, current affairs and local information in Punjabi. (AM 530)

CHINESE

With the completion of the Canadian Pacific Railway in 1885, thousands of Chinese labourers became unemployed. Almost immediately the Canadian government created a "head tax" to further slow Chinese immigration on the grounds that it would take jobs away from white people.

Some railway workers drifted east to Toronto. Encountering discriminatory hiring practices, they began opening their own businesses. By the 1920s hundreds of Chinese restaurants, grocery stores and hand laundries existed in the southern fringe of the Ward, where Chinese males outnumbered females 10 to one.

This original Chinatown was expropriated in the 1950s to build Toronto's new City Hall. Relocated businesses and new immigrants alike concentrated their economic activity around Dundas West and Spadina Avenue. Known as "new" Chinatown, it became a major tourist attraction.

Spurred by Communist China's impending takeover, residents of

Did you know. . .

that in 2001, Statistics Canada counted 135 visible minority neighbourhoods in Toronto, up from six nationwide in 1981?

Gay Toronto

Of course there have been gay Torontonians since the town was founded. The single mobilizing force for the gay community, however, were the 1981 police raids on four bathhouses. The first mass demonstration by the gay community ensued, and the municipal government commissioned a report that formally recognized Toronto's gays and lesbians as a community for the first time.

Pride Toronto has been around since the 1970s and an annual celebration since 1981. In the early days, there were Gay Days picnics at Hanlan's Point, moving later to Cawthra Park. In 1991 city council proclaimed the first Pride Day, and attendance reached 80,000.

Pride Week is now one of the major arts-and-cultural festivals in the country and, with an estimated attendance of more than one million people, one of the largest Pride celebrations in the world. Held every June, Pride Week is one of only eight officially designated City of Toronto "signature events." It is recognized as one of the Top 50 Festivals in Ontario by Festivals and Events Ontario and has been given the Best Festival in Canada Award by the Canadian Special Event Industry two years in a row.

Toronto has two main centres of gay life, one well-defined and with a long history, the other more recent and too dispersed to qualify as a "village." The more historic area is bounded by Yonge, Jarvis, Maitland and Carlton streets, long ago the estate of Alexander Wood, an Upper Canada merchant and magistrate who was at the centre of a gay sex scandal in 1810. His lands became known as Molly Wood's Bush in the early 19th century, "molly" being slang for homosexual at the time.

In 2005 a statue of Wood was placed at the corner of Church and Alexander streets (the latter named for Wood), honouring him as a forefather of Toronto's contemporary gay community. Today the Church and Wellesley area is the public venue for many gay activities, including bars, restaurants, shops and community organizations. Same-sex marriages have been legal in Toronto since 2003, making it a major gay tourist destination.

Hong Kong began a new wave of immigration in the 1980s. Many settled outside the downtown core in suburbs such as Markham, Mississauga and Agincourt, where shiny new malls operate entirely in Cantonese and Mandarin. The population of ethnic Chinese now exceeds 283,000.

TAKE 5 DAN YASHINSKY'S TOP FIVE
TORONTO STORYTELLING DESTINATIONS

Storytelling is enjoying an international renaissance, and Toronto is one of its major centres. Dan Yashinsky has been at the heart of the T.O. scene since 1978. He is the author of *Suddenly They Heard Footsteps: Storytelling for the Twenty-first Century* and the founder of the Toronto Festival of Storytelling, and he has performed and taught at festivals throughout Canada and around the world. In 1999 he was awarded Toronto's Jane Jacobs Prize for his work. "It's no surprise Toronto is such fertile ground for the oral tradition, old and new," he says. "Toronto is a crossroads city, one of the greatest since Byzantium. What do people bring to the crossroads? Their stories!"

1. **Kensington Market:** In 1978 I started hosting 1,001 Friday Nights of Storytelling at a little café called Gaffers on Kensington Avenue. Gaffers is long gone, but you can still catch the spirit of Toronto's early storytelling movement by walking the streets of Kensington Market. I enjoy walking there with my ears open, soaking up the accents, bargaining and political discussions that echo in the stores and on the sidewalks.

2. **1,001 Friday Nights of Storytelling:** The world's longest-running weekly storytelling gathering now happens every Friday night at the Innis College cafeteria at U of T. The host offers a talking stick to whoever has a word-of-mouth story to tell. There's no planned program, every evening is unique and many people come just to listen. Someone once commented that, with its candle-lit atmosphere and

In Chinatown the shops and grocery stores, with their celebrated braised ducks hanging in the windows, still remain. But most of the famed restaurants along Dundas Street, including the barbecue shops located below grade, have closed since 2000. A variety of East Asian immigrants have settled the area, and Chinatown has become noticeably more Vietnamese in character.

sense of community, the evening is like witnessing the beginning of human civilization.

3. **Lillian H. Smith Library:** This wonderful library at Huron and College has several special collections, including storytelling, puppetry and science fiction, plus the world-famous Osborne collection of children's books. All storytellers, whether professional or amateur, visit this library to research storytelling traditions and collections from around the world. Joan Bodger, a founder of the Toronto storytelling movement, wrote the library into *The Crack in the Teacup: The Life of an Old Woman Steeped in Stories*, one of the best books about storytelling written in the last hundred years.

4. **The Barns:** Wychwood Artscape Barns is the headquarters of Storytelling Toronto. It hosts talks, performances, workshops and an annual festival, and it's now in one of Toronto's most incredible reno jobs. The complex of derelict streetcar barns was saved from demolition and transformed into an arts centre that opened in 2008. It also houses a weekly farmers' market, studios and performance spaces.

5. **Toronto Cafés:** Storytellers are hunters and gatherers of the spoken word. I do a lot of my writing in cafés, keeping an ear half-cocked to the conversations around me. Some of the best cafés for this kind of word-collecting: I Deal Coffee (Nassau Street in Kensington Market); Dooney's (Bloor and Borden); World Class Bakers (St. Clair at Christie); Ellington's (St. Clair at Winona); and The Common (College and Dufferin).

ITALIANS

Toronto's pre-1940 colony of Italians numbered less than 16,000, but when federal immigration policy relaxed in 1950, the Italian community rushed to sponsor relatives to come to Canada. They wrote their *paesani*, or fellow countrymen, with advice, offered loans for the voyage, helped steer them through bureaucracy and often provided them with housing and jobs upon their arrival. Toronto was undergoing a post-war building boom and needed stonemasons, cement workers, carpenters, plasterers, bricklayers and labourers. Italian immigrants were ready and willing to fill the gaps.

In 1960 five Italian construction workers were killed while building the Yonge Street subway line. The Hogg's Hollow disaster was a wake-up call to thousands of immigrants working in unsafe conditions. The tragedy spurred them to unionize, instigate strikes and force improved conditions. As late as 1971, almost one-third of Italian male workers were employed in construction trades, increasingly for Italian-owned companies.

Italians created social clubs and banquet halls to ease the alienation associated with immigration. Known for their elaborate wedding feasts and ceremonies, the venues became central to the maintenance of kinship networks with their *paesani*.

Like other immigrant groups, the newcomers settled downtown first, beginning in the Ward, then moving along to College Street (now the area known as Little Italy) and eventually to Corso Italia, centred around St. Clair West. Today many Italians live in the suburbs, with a large contingent in Woodbridge.

Did you know. . .

that Toronto's 911 emergency service can respond in more than 150 languages?

Bio Johnny Lombardi

Born in the Ward (reputedly on the kitchen table) within a stone's throw of today's Eaton Centre, Johnny Lombardi was a self-made success who founded two Toronto institutions, CHIN Multicultural Radio and the CHIN International Picnic, and became the face of multiculturalism long before it was a buzzword or official government policy.

The music-loving son of Italian immigrants, Lombardi was ambitious and energetic from the start. He grew up in Little Italy during the 1920s and '30s, shining shoes outside music halls as a boy. By age 14, he had formed his own band and gradually built a career playing popular dance music, a path that detoured when he went overseas with the Canadian army during World War II.

In the 1950s, back in Little Italy, Lombardi started a grocery business that catered to the incoming wave of Italian immigrants, importing specialty items then unavailable in the white-bread city. Soon he was bringing in more than just food. As an impresario, Lombardi sponsored a series of Italian singers, which took place at first in small venues and later in the venerable Massey Hall and Roy Thomson Hall.

It was an easy segue to radio, and the popularity of Lombardi's one-hour Italian show on CHUM and CKFH gave him the confidence to launch the multicultural CHIN in 1966 from atop his College Street grocery store. Lombardi felt the station was a vital link in connecting the Italian community. "Many may have gone back to Italy if CHIN wasn't around to help make them feel at home," he once said.

Lombardi's love of music and all things Italian never diminished, and he was a tireless organizer and fundraiser for philanthropic causes, including the world's largest free picnic, the CHIN International Picnic. He continued his enthusiastic cultural endeavours until his death in 2002 at age 86. Piazza Lombardi at the corner of Grace and College streets honours this pioneer with two plaques and a smiling sculpture.

PORTUGUESE

Portuguese immigration began in the mid-1950s, when young men received contracts to work as railway workers and farmhands in rural Canada. Most who arrived in Ontario came from the Azores and Madeira Island; they eventually ended up in Toronto.

Sousa's Restaurant in Kensington Market was a magnet for new arrivals seeking a sympathetic ear and a place to stay. Once established, the young men sent for their wives and children, settling in Kensington Market and Alexandra Park. The greatest aspiration of these immigrants was to own a home that would provide them with the sense of security and belonging they so desperately desired.

As the Portuguese population grew, so did the number of businesses they owned, and newcomers were directed toward them. These included bakeries, grocery stores, fish dealers, travel agencies, driving schools and real estate agencies.

Portuguese immigration peaked by 1970. More than 170,000 Portuguese—one-third of Canada's entire Portuguese population— now live in the GTA. Little Portugal, located to the west and north of Trinty-Bellwoods Park in west-end Toronto, is one of the city's most visible ethnic neighbourhoods. The enclave contains most of the community's social, cultural, commercial and religious institutions and is home to 12,000 Portuguese-Canadians.

SOUTH ASIANS

Canada's current immigration laws favour professionals and skilled tradespeople. Many South Asians have these qualifications, as well as the desire to improve their economic fortunes. As a result, Toronto has become a magnet for emigrants from the Indian subcontinent. More than 300,000 South Asians now live in the GTA.

Religion is an essential touchstone for South Asian immigrants. Toronto has 63 Hindu temples, each a bulwark for the ever-growing Hindu community. Sikh men, with their beards and brightly coloured turbans, are the most visible minority group in the city. Toronto is also home to Canada's largest population of Pakistani immigrants, who are chiefly Muslim.

The Gerrard India Bazaar on Gerrard Street East is a key gathering spot for South Asians. Little India, as it is also known, offers an exotic display of sights, sounds, tastes and aromas and over 100 shops serving the interests of people of the Indian subcontinent. A mark of the harmony that exists between the cultures that flock to the bazaar was the holding of a joint Diwali (Hindu Festival of Lights) and EID (Muslim end of Ramadan) celebration, when the two holidays coincided in October of 2006.

Bio Michael Ondaatje

In his first novel, *In the Skin of a Lion*, published in 1987, Michael Ondaatje gives a face to the many immigrants who contributed to building early Toronto. The book is an exposé of the immigrant condition. "It is a novel about the wearing and the removal of masks; the shedding of skin, the transformations and translations of identity," Ondaatje has said.

The central character is a Macedonian immigrant who works on ambitious projects such as the Bloor Street Viaduct and the RC Harris Water Treatment Plant. The story shows how labourers toiled on such architectural wonders while remaining on the extreme fringe of mainstream society.

Ondaatje is best known for his later novels *The English Patient* and *Anil's Ghost*. The former, published in 1992, won the Governor General's Award and the Booker Prize for fiction and was adapted into a movie that won the 1996 Oscar for Best Picture.

Ondaatje immigrated to Toronto in 1962 from Sri Lanka via London and Montreal. Still, the city can make a strong claim on him—not only because he graduated from the University of Toronto, taught at York University and did intricate research on historical Toronto but also because he survived on falafels served up by El Basha restaurant, then located near Spadina and Bloor,

CARIBBEAN-CANADIANS

In 1967 new liberal immigration laws combined with tighter restrictions on immigration to Britain created a surge of Caribbean migration to Toronto. These newcomers came from English-speaking islands, particularly Barbados, Jamaica and Trinidad and Tobago.

Newly arrived immigrants from Trinidad formed a steel band that played at Expo 67 in Montreal. Returning to Toronto, they initiated the creation of eight bands that played before a thousand spectators that same summer. The concert is considered the first Caribana, modelled after Trinidad's Carnivale, which has now grown to be the largest Caribbean festival in North America. Canadian hip-hop culture is centred in Toronto and has been significantly influenced by the rhythms and styles of Jamaican and Bahamian music.

Immigrants from the Caribbean often settled around Eglinton and Vaughan Road or the Bathurst and Bloor area. As these zones became crowded, many dispersed and mixed with the general population. The Jamaican community has tended to gather in distinct neighbourhoods such as Rexdale, Lawrence Heights, Malvern (in Scarborough) and the Jane-Finch area, which has one of the highest proportions of gangs, sole-supported families and low-income earners of any Toronto community.

FILIPINOS

Since 1985 the Philippines has been one of the most important sources of immigration to Toronto. Since that year, the population has grown from 35,000 to well over 100,000.

Many young female Filipino workers come to Toronto under the strict discipline of the Domestic Worker Programme. Working as nannies has

Did you know...

that Toronto is home to 22.9 percent of all visible minority persons in Canada and 42.4 percent of visible minority persons in Ontario?

helped these women gain a foothold in their new country. Even college-educated Filipinos were attracted, because they could earn more working in lower-status jobs in Canada than they could as professionals at home.

Newcomers settled first where inexpensive housing could be found near Catholic churches and job sites such as hospitals and office buildings. Two popular communities for new immigrants were the Queen and Jameson neighbourhood and St. Jamestown, a cluster of high-rise apartments near Sherbourne and Wellesley streets. Here, nannies and nurses often lived two or three to an apartment to save money. It was common for the young immigrants of this family-oriented culture to sponsor parents and other relatives to join them in Toronto.

Weblinks

Help! (In Languages Other than English)

www.toronto.ca/immigration/translations_imm.htm
Selected city services focus on immigration and settlement issues, in 17 non-English languages.

Access Toronto, In Your Own Language

www.toronto.ca/accesstoronto/publications.htm
Download four informational brochures about city politics, services and structure in such languages as Chinese, French, Greek, Italian, Polish, Portuguese, Punjabi, Spanish, Tagalog, Tamil and Vietnamese.

Eat Ethnic

www.toronto-restaurants.com
Toronto's most extensive online restaurant directory and guide is organized alphabetically by cuisine and includes regularly updated reviews.

Urban Geography

Twenty thousand years ago, the area of present-day downtown Toronto was covered by an ice sheet four times higher than the CN Tower. Twelve thousand years ago, it was under water, the ice-blocked St. Lawrence not yet draining the glacial Lake Iroquois.

Today the city sprawls north of Lake Ontario across a shelf of sedimentary rock. Its generally flat landscape was left behind by the Iroquois (it was essentially an enlargement of current Lake Ontario) when it finally receded about 11,000 years ago. The ancient shoreline is still recognizable in the city, in the ridge that runs roughly east-west north of Davenport Road (it eventually joins the Scarborough Bluffs in the east).

Water—both the Don River and the lake itself—also helped create the city's excellent natural harbour. Sediment that eroded from the Scarborough Bluffs gradually formed shallow water and then a long curving spit of marshland east of the Don, which helped shelter York's early shipping. Today, thanks to a massive landfill project, the area has become Toronto's Leslie Street Spit, a five-kilometre-long peninsula and urban-wilderness area that protects the busy harbour from wind and weather in the east.

Toronto may be without a mountainous backdrop or an iconic

Mount Royal, but it is not without its own characteristic geographic feature—one that's cut *into* the land. Dozens of ravines and valleys thread through the city, carved by the streams and rivers that drain into the lake. Left largely undeveloped, they add significantly to the city's green canopy. Many also continue to fulfill a longstanding role: aboriginal people, the French, the English, and current Torontonians have all used these rivers and valleys for canoe routes, roads and pathways.

Historically, the city's ravines helped dictate how the city grew. They provided industry and farmers with access to water, and the alluvial soil of the largest valleys was easier to work for crops. Today they merge industrial "urbania" with the natural environment, providing places to enjoy nature. Downtown Toronto may sometimes be called a concrete jungle—it has the second-highest concentration of high-rises in North America, behind New York City—but its ravines and parks counter the grey with a significant amount of green.

The pre-eminent natural presence in the city remains Lake Ontario, which is how Torontonians continue to orient themselves, consciously or not. As surely as the sun rises in the east, if you're in Toronto and facing the lake, you know you're looking south.

LATITUDE AND LONGITUDE

Toronto is located at 43° 39' North latitude and 79° 23' West longitude, roughly as far north of the equator as Bucharest (Romania), Nice (France) and Urumqi (China) and on a north-south line with Guayaquil (Ecuador), Panama City (Panama) and Lima (Peru).

LAND AREA

Ottawa	2,796 sq. km
Hamilton	1,117 sq. km
Toronto	**630 sq. km**
Winnipeg	464 sq. km
Montreal	365 sq. km
Vancouver	115 sq. km

ECOLOGICAL FOOTPRINT

An ecological footprint is a calculation that estimates the area of the Earth's productive land and water required to supply the resources and absorb the wastes of an individual or group.

- Average number of hectares used to sustain one Canadian, or the size of their ecological footprint: 7.25
- Montrealer: 6.89
- Torontonian: 7.36
- Vancouverite: 7.71
- Calgarian: 9.86

Source: Federation of Canadian Municipalities

SHORELINE

- Toronto's shoreline length as the crow flies: 43 km
- Shoreline length including bays and islands: 138 km

ELEVATION

- Lowest elevation: 76.5 m above sea level on the shoreline of Lake Ontario
- Highest elevation: 270 m above sea level, located near the York University grounds in the city's north end

Did you know. . .

that in the 1870s the King and Simcoe intersection was known as "Salvation–Legislation–Education–Damnation" for the buildings on the corners? Salvation for St. Andrew's Presbyterian Church (on the southeast corner), legislation for Government House (southwest corner), education for Upper Canada College (northwest corner) and damnation for the British Tavern (northeast corner). Only the original "Salvation" remains today.

TAKE 5 FIVE OLDEST BUILDINGS
IN TORONTO

1. **Scadding Cabin**, now located at Exhibition Place, built in 1794 by the Queen's York Rangers
2. **Guild Log Cabin**, on Guildwood Parkway, built in 1795
3. **John Cox Cottage**, at 469 Broadview Ave., built ca. 1807
4. **Gibraltar Point Lighthouse**, on the Toronto Islands, built in 1808
5. **Fort York**, Blockhouse No. 2 at 100 Garrison Rd., built in 1813

HERE AND THERE

Toronto is:

- 399 km from Ottawa
- 554 km from Montreal
- 1,929 km from Halifax
- 4,537 km from Vancouver
- 3,491 km from Calgary
- 130 km from the U.S. border
- 831 km from New York City

Source: The Travel Network of Canada

Did you know. . .

that more than one-third of Toronto's area (34.8 percent) is residential? Other large chunks include industrial (7.8 percent), institutional (schools, universities, churches, cemeteries, at 7.3 percent) and commercial (2.3 percent).

Jacob's Ladder

When Jane Jacobs moved with her family from New York City to Toronto in 1968 (she was intent on keeping her sons from being drafted into the Vietnam War), she was already a well-known and internationally respected thinker. Her activist opposition in New York that she used to defeat the Lower Manhattan Expressway she brought to Toronto. She lived by the dictum clearly stated in her first book, published in 1961 and entitled *The Death and Life of Great American Cities*. Cities succeed (or fail), she said, because of the people who live in them, not the politicians who claim to run them.

And she loved her new city. "As a relatively recent transplant from New York, I am frequently asked whether I find Toronto sufficiently exciting," she said. "I find it almost too exciting. The suspense is scary. Here is the most hopeful and healthy city in North America, still unmangled, still with options." For the next four decades, she continued to be an outspoken critic of top-down urban decision-making in her new Canadian home. She was a huge support to those whose vision of the city included keeping its neighbourhoods human-scaled.

In the early 1970s Jacobs helped lead the "Stop Spadina" campaign. The proposed expressway would, she felt, "Los Angelize" some of Toronto's liveliest neighborhoods, including her own (the Annex). She spoke and wrote in favour of more autonomy for the City of Toronto and broad revisions to Toronto's Official Plan, and against the Ontario Hydro empire and expanding the Toronto Island Airport.

Her importance to Toronto went even deeper than her influence on public policy. She became the unofficial conscience and champion for downtown neighbourhoods. She marched, she gave speeches, she gave advice, she hung out in her neighbourhood. Her interest and influence in the city continued until her death in 2006, at 89.

In 2007, Mayor David Miller proclaimed May 4 (her birthday) Jane Jacobs Day. It is now celebrated (by a series of "Jane's Walks") every year in Toronto, as it is in more than a dozen other cities and towns across Canada and the U.S. The Jane Jacobs Prize has been awarded annually since 1999 to an unsung community hero, and there is talk of making space for a Piazza Jane Jacobs somewhere in her adopted city.

TAKE 5 JOHN SEWELL'S TOP FIVE
TORONTO BUILDINGS NOT TO MISS

A former Toronto mayor, John Sewell is also a well-known activist and a writer. He was born in Toronto, raised in the Beach and educated at the University of Toronto and its law school. Sewell was first elected to Toronto city council in 1969, a champion of such causes as protecting neighbourhoods and heritage structures, improving public transit and helping to increase the stock of affordable housing for low-income households. He served as mayor from 1978 to 1980, when he was known for both his informal style and intensity, and as chair of the Metro Toronto Housing Authority. He continues to write and speak on a range of urban issues.

1. **University College** (University of Toronto main campus): Designed by Frederick Cumberland, this extraordinary building incorporates many of the critic John Ruskin's ideas about Gothic architecture. Built in the late 1850s, and faithfully rebuilt after a fire 10 years later, it is marvelously organic—full of stone and wooden carvings, with no two columns inside or outside the building the same and with stained glass designs that vary from room to room. The detailing is a delight, from the roundels in the west gallery to the dragons at the foot of the staircases.

2. **R.C. Harris waterworks** (Queen Street East at Neville Park): Built in the late 1920s, this elegant Art Deco structure has gained a mythic place in the city's imagination (see Michael Ondaatje's novel *In the Skin of the Lion*). It is named after the Toronto engineer and commissioner of public works who is responsible for many other public buildings, also of notable architectural interest, built during the 1930s. Sadly, the inside of the building is not open to the public.

3. **New City Hall:** Designed by Viljo Revell in the 1960s and looking somewhat like a giant sculpture, this is the structure that made Toronto a contemporary city. Nathan Phillips Square at its base, the city's first space dedicated to public gatherings, has become a focal point for rallies, demonstrations and celebrations. To the east is Old City Hall, which was opened in 1899, a wonder saved from demolition in the 1960s; to the west is even older Osgoode Hall, the seat of the Law Society and two senior Ontario courts.

4. **401 Richmond St. West** (just east of Spadina): Inside this unprepossessing 19th-century factory building is a potpourri of artists, innovators, performers and creative businesses. Margie Zeidler, daughter of prominent Toronto architect Eberhard Zeidler, had the idea in the early 1990s to create a space to contain the mix of uses that Jane Jacobs would be pleased with. (She was.) "401," as people call it, showcases the innovative side of the city; cultural events are often held here.

5. **Four Seasons Centre for the Performing Arts** (Queen and University): Designed by A. J. Diamond, this elegant building is a fine example of the modest and reserved "Toronto style," which itself owes much to Diamond's work in the city over his long career. The building stands out as perhaps the best designed of the five big cultural initiatives of the first decade of the millennium. Also on the list: Royal Ontario Museum, Ontario College of Art and Design, Art Gallery of Ontario and the Royal Conservatory of Music.

Neighbourhood ABCs

Annex: A downtown area just north of the main University of Toronto campus offering good eats, an eclectic mix of clothing boutiques, bookstores and coffee shops.

Beaches, The: The area north of the sandy beach east of downtown. It is known either as "the Beach," which many residents will assure you is its proper historical tag, or "the Beaches," a more widely used neighbourhood name, particularly by non-residents.

Bluffs: The Scarborough Bluffs, east of downtown, stretch for about 14 km along the Lake Ontario shoreline from West Hill to the eastern edge of the Beach. They offer some of the city's best views of Lake Ontario.

Cabbagetown: Known for the longest continuous line of preserved Victorian housing in North America, this east Toronto neighbourhood's name refers to the Irish and Macedonian immigrants who began arriving there in the 1840s and grew cabbages in their front yards.

High Park: Named by John Howard circa 1837, who built his estate there and later donated the land to the city, Toronto's largest park covers 161 hectares on the highest point of land above Humber Bay. It's surrounded by comfortable mixed neighbourhoods, and the park itself is a mecca for people from all over the city, especially in summer.

The Island: With four beaches, three yacht clubs, one canoe club, a children's amusement park and a small residential community, "the Island" is actually a chain of seven islands across from the downtown core, officially called the Toronto Islands.

Junction: Prior to European settlement, two Iroquois trails intersected in the area of what is now Keele and Dundas streets. The name took on additional meaning later, because the area was near the junction of four railway lines known as the West Toronto Diamond.

Kensington: A distinctive multicultural neighbourhood in downtown Toronto, and since 2006 a National Historic Site, Kensington has one of the city's oldest and most famous markets. Eclectic food and clothing shops, cafés and fresh-produce vendors line the area's narrow streets, which visitors travel mostly by foot or bicycle.

The Lakeshore: Lakeshore Boulevard is an east-west route running along most of Toronto's waterfront, flanked by a walkway next to the lake in large stretches.

Leslie Street Spit: An urban wilderness area, the Spit is a 5 km peninsula built by construction landfill that juts into the lake east of the Toronto Islands. Begun in the late 1950s as a breakwater for harbour expansion, the site is now popular with cyclists, birdwatchers, landscape artists and Sunday-afternoon strollers.

Queen's Park: Torontonians often use this term interchangeably with "Government of Ontario" because the provincial-legislature buildings are located in Queen's Park, just north of College Street and University Avenue.

Square, The: Now officially "Toronto Life Square," this flashy Yonge and Dundas destination, with its bright lights and big billboards, is like Times Square's little brother. It has become a venue for outdoor local entertainment, various types of celebrations and activist demonstrations.

West Queen West: Toronto's art-and-design district is located exactly where its name suggests—the western part of Queen Street West—and is on the cutting edge of style. Trendy galleries, artists, clothing shops and cafés distinguish the area.

Yorkville: Fusing historic charm and modern seduction, this is Toronto's upscale style neighbourhood. It has designer boutiques, fashionable restaurants, world-class galleries and the city's first five-star hotel.

THREE RIVERS RUN THROUGH IT

The city's three biggest rivers are the Humber, the Don and the Rouge. Taking their tributaries into account, they total about 307 km of running water, which, of course, all ends up in Lake Ontario—and, yes, eventually in the Atlantic Ocean.

The largest of the rivers is the Humber, which has two main branches; one that runs about 100 km from the Niagara Escarpment, the other starting in the northeast in Lake St. George near Aurora. In total it is fed by more than 750 creeks and tributaries.

The Humber has witnessed three waves of native settlement, the earliest dating to 10,000 BC. The Humber was the southern portion of

TAKE 5 FIVE MUST-SEE OUTDOOR SCULPTURES

1. **Gould on a Bench:** The life-size sculpture of Gould by Canadian sculptor Ruth Abernethy, based on a photo by Don Hunstein, sits on a bench outside CBC's HQ on Front Street West.

2. **Roman Column:** Yes, it's a real one. The column in Nathan Phillips' Square dates to 300–400 AD. It was quarried in Egypt and presented to the city in 1957 by Umberto Tupini, then mayor of Rome.

3. **The Endless Bench:** Outside The Hospital for Sick Children on University Avenue is a bronze circular bench into which the artist carved almost 500 messages of love, hope and inspiration. Featuring two children playing and two women chatting, it was donated by artist Lea Vivot in memory of her son Morris.

4. **The Pasture:** Seven bronze cows by Joe Fafard "graze" between the TD towers. It's a tranquil spot (the buildings shield the noise) to escape the hustle and bustle of the financial district.

5. **Native Peoples:** This bronze group of men, women, children and animals (a bear, an otter, a wolf and an eagle) by sculptor Abraham Anghikin pays tribute to the First Nations of Canada. It's located in North York at 3200 Dufferin St.

the Carrying Place trail used by native peoples and early Europeans to travel between Lakes Ontario and Simcoe. Emptying into Humber Bay west of Toronto Harbour, the Humber remains largely free of industrialization and is now parkland for much of its inter-urban length, a transformation sped by the disastrous flooding brought about by Hurricane Hazel. For its significance to Toronto, the Humber earned a national Heritage River designation in 1999.

More critical to York's early development was the much shorter Don River, at about 38 km long, which lies in a broad valley that stretches to 400 m wide at the Bloor Street Viaduct, evidence of its ancient roots as a glacial river. The Don also has two main tributaries, the East and West branches, which meet about 7 km north of the lakeshore. It does empty into the harbour and was used by the first Europeans more heavily than the Humber because it was closer to the early community.

Named by Simcoe after Yorkshire's River Don, it was the site of several early mills and, later, industrial and infrastructure development; its egress into the lake was also diverted into concrete channels and it became quite polluted in the process. Ongoing efforts to clean it up began in the late 1980s and are enjoying some success, although it still often has a murky flow.

Further to the east is the 250 km Rouge River, a two-tier system of Little Rouge and Rouge River that serves as the boundary between Toronto and Pickering. It is the centrepiece waterway of the spectacular 50 sq. km Rouge Park, a largely undeveloped protected area. Unlike Toronto's other two main rivers, the Rouge functions naturally, rising over its floodplain as nature dictates.

Did you know...

that when the CN tower was under construction, the schedule of "Olga"—the Sikorsky helicopter that lifted sections of it into place—was published in the papers so people could watch?

THREE LOST RIVERS OF TORONTO

1. **Garrison Creek:** Buried since the mid-1920s, Garrison Creek ran 7.7 km from roughly the Dufferin and St. Clair intersection down to Lake Ontario near Old Fort York.

2. **Taddle Creek:** Also known as Brewery Creek and the Little Don River, Taddle was buried in stages between 1860 and 1886. The University of Toronto's Philosopher's Walk follows Taddle Creek's ravine, and a small bit of the water still surfaces in Trinity Square.

Tower Tales

Interpret it as you will—a symbol of Toronto's giant wannabe ego, anyone?—but Canadian National, the actual creators of the Toronto skyline's unmistakable phallic punctuation mark, swears it was built as an official demonstration of "the strength of Canadian industry." Regardless of why it was built, for 31 glorious years— until Dubai oil money created something larger—when *Guinness World Records* and the curious the world over wanted to know which was the world's tallest freestanding building, the answer was the CN Tower.

Officially opened in 1976, the CN Tower tops out at 554.3 m (181 storeys), twice the height of the Eiffel Tower. It is clearly the most recognizable structure on the Toronto skyline and a common point of reference. Now three decades old and counting, it is more a familiar workhorse than an awe-inspiring wonder. And although more striking, albeit not taller, structures have lessened her effect, she's still something to behold.

It took 40 months to build the structure, and on a clear day it's visible from the other side of the lake. Many who can remember its early years also recall the poster that appeared around the city at the time. It showed the radius of the tower's "fall zone" and put

3. **Castle Frank Brook:** Formed from three small streams in the Dufferin and Lawrence area, Castle Frank Brook entered the Don via three ravines—Cedarvale, Nordheimer and Rosedale Valley—just south of the Bloor Viaduct. It was named for the summer home of Sir John Graves Simcoe.

the size of the thing in eerie ground-level perspective.

These days about two million people a year, almost all out-of-towners, take the turbo elevator to the observation and entertainment decks. In the glass-floored room you can look directly down to the ground while standing on a mere 2.5 inches of glass. Those who prefer the long view and a real floor eat in the 360 Restaurant, which takes 72 minutes to complete a leisurely revolution.

The CN Tower has been courted by a few oddballs over the years. In 1980 Donn Reynolds yodelled from the Skypod roof for almost seven and a half hours. In 1986 "Spider Dan" Goodwin scaled up the outside via the stairway windows, twice on the same day. And in 1999 a visiting New Yorker ascended the 1,899 steps—yes, you can walk up or down—in just under an hour on a pogo stick, no less.

Nonsense aside, the tower's function as a place to mount transmitters has been of exceptional service to Torontonians, guaranteeing good reception even in the skyscrapered streets of downtown, making her a loyal and trusted giant companion.

GETTIN' 'ROUND

When John Graves Simcoe ordered the troops to start hacking byways into the forest, he set the straight-as-an-arrow pattern for Toronto's urban grid. Subsequent surveyors followed his lead, continuing the march across the landscape in three directions—north, east and west—in an orderly fashion that laid out the concession lines and farmland packages that would be later swallowed by urban expansion. The exceptions—the unexpected curves in Toronto's generally bowling-alley straight main roads—occur where natural features could not be avoided: escarpments, ravines, and rivers (surface or now buried).

Yonge Street is the city's defining north-south artery. It is flanked on the east by Bayview and the west by Spadina, Bathurst and

TAKE 5 CHARLES PACHTER'S FIVE
MOOSE-VIEWING LOCATIONS

A celebrated artist—he has received the Order of Canada and the Queen's Jubilee Medal—Charles Pachter was born in Toronto and educated at the University of Toronto, the Cranbook Academy of Art and the Sorbonne. Over a long career, he has created images that have become humorous pop icons of contemporary Canadian culture. They include his take on Queen Elizabeth II and the great Canadian moose (often together) and the Maple Leaf flag. Pachter has lived and worked for many years beside historic Grange Park in downtown Toronto and has a keen interest in Upper Canadian history. His steel-and-granite moose installations appear around the city.

1. **"Mooseconstrue"** at Harbord Street and St. George Street.
2. **"Moosedemeanour"** in the Courtyard Pond at U of T's Graduate House at Harbord and Spadina.
3. **"Moose on a Roof"** atop the Moose Factory at 22 Grange Ave.
4. **"Inaugural Moose"** at City Hall Plaza for the citywide Moose in the City event in 2000.
5. **"Marilyn Moose"** and **"Mel Moose"** in front of Old City Hall.

TAKE 5 TORONTO'S (AND CANADA'S)
FIVE TALLEST OFFICE TOWERS

1. **First Bank Tower:** 298 m, built in 1975
2. **Scotia Plaza:** 275 m, built in 1988
3. **Commerce Court West:** 239 m, built in 1972
4. **Canada Trust Tower:** 226 m, built in 1990
5. **Toronto-Dominion Bank Tower:** 223 m, built in 1967

Source: Tall Buildings

University/Avenue Road, all of which run to the city's northern boundary at Steeles Avenue and beyond. A series of east-west thoroughfares march northward from the lake: Front, Queen, King, Bloor/Danforth, St. Clair, Eglinton and Lawrence, to name a few.

Like most major North American cities, and despite an excellent transit system, Toronto is still ruled by the car, so expressways ring or cut the city, feeding commuters into and out of the downtown core. The Gardiner Expressway runs along the lake from downtown west, the 401 slices through the city in the north and the 427 (in the west) and the Don Valley Parkway in the east connect north with south.

The Toronto Transit Commission (TTC) is the mass-transit alternative for the car-less. Its three main subway lines—Bloor/Danforth, Yonge and University—are relatively clean, and even at rush hour usually orderly and polite. Several subway stations are terminal points for bus and streetcar lines that fan out on the surface. By car or transit, Toronto is generally an easy and safe city to move around in.

Did you know. . .

that at a quarry in the Don Valley, geologists discovered nine distinct layers revealing three past three glaciations dating back 120,000 years?

WHERE WATER MEETS LAND

Toronto's downtown waterfront was long the city's industrial and man-ufacturing heart. Beginning in the mid-1850s, the area was known for grimy factories that burned coal to produce steam power. Since coal came from Pennsylvania by ship, Torontonians built their factories as close to the water as possible. The waterfront was actually moved south-ward, created by landfill, but much of it remained an industrial zone for well over a century. Railways and roads laced across the area, further separating the bustling non-industrial downtown from its harbour.

Today much of this industrial area is being taken over by living space but with mixed results. A curtain wall of condos stretches along the Esplanade south of the railway tracks, and both it and the Gardiner Expressway, built in the 1950s, block street-level views of the lake. Anyone heading to the waterfront on foot from downtown has to trudge through dark smoggy underpasses or traverse the windswept plain below the CN Tower. Downtown residents who care about the lake—and if you live uptown, it does slip from your radar—find the situation deplorable and are happy for good spots in which they can enjoy life on the waterfront. Here are a few preferred waterfront destinations:

- Bluffers Park: A good picnic area at the foot of the Scarborough Bluffs.
- The Eastern Beaches: Especially in July, when you can catch live jazz, fusion, R&B at the 10-day free Beaches International Jazz Festival.
- Tommy Thompson Park: Extensive wetlands, meadows and forests cover this park on the Leslie Street Spit, which also has a long bik-ing/hiking trail.
- Ontario Place: Entertainment central on three man-made islands across from the CNE grounds: concerts, water slides, rides and the world's first permanent IMAX theatre.
- Exhibition Place: Almost every Toronto kid can sing "Let's Go to the Ex," but Exhibition Place is no longer just for the Canadian

National Exhibition. There are more than 192 acres of parkland, historical buildings, and trade show/exhibition centres. Together they attract 4.5 million visitors a year, particularly to indoor events such as the Royal Agricultural Winter Fair, the Toronto International Boat Show, the Toronto Sportsmen's Show and the One of a Kind Craft Show.

• Humber Bay Park: Created from 5.1 million cubic metres of landfill, this two-section park has fly-casting and model boat ponds, wild-flower meadows, recreation and picnic facilities and a butterfly habitat. The eastern side has Toronto's memorial to the victims of the 1985 Air India Flight bombing; many of the 329 killed in the 1985 disaster were from the GTA.

Source: City of Toronto

TAKE 5 FIVE LAKE ONTARIO
FACTS

1. It is the smallest Great Lake (surface area) but the eighth-largest body of water in North America and the 14th largest lake in the world.
2. It drains an area of 90,130 sq. km and has the second-deepest average depth behind Lake Superior.
3. Ninety-three percent of it flows out through the St. Lawrence; the rest of its water loss occurs through evaporation.
4. Its depth and southern Ontario's moderate climate, which is warmed by predominant southwesterlies, means Lake Ontario rarely freezes in the winter.
5. In 1615, Etienne Brulé was the first European to sail its waters.

Sources: Government of Ontario and Canadian Encyclopedia

T.O. BEACHES

The city's Waterfront Beach Management puts summer beach visits to their 11 supervised beaches at over two million visitors annually. The beaches—six of which have been awarded International Blue Flag Status, the international designation for safety and cleanliness—are open during the summer months.

The Longest in the World

Toronto likes to claim that Yonge Street is the longest street in the world. It's true that the pavement does begin at Lake Ontario and end at Rainy River, some 1,896 km away near the Minnesota border.

Considered Toronto's main north-south street, it was named for Sir George Yonge, an 18th-century British Secretary for War who was (no surprise) an expert on Roman roads. Construction began in 1793 in York, and the road, built for trade and military defence, opened three years later.

Yonge divides Toronto into its east and west halves. It has many key junctions, including Yonge and Dundas, Yonge and Queen, and Yonge and Eglinton, and shopping districts. It was the natural choice for the route of the city's first subway line, and it has been the traditional gathering place for public celebrations.

But is it really the world's longest street? Not anymore. Yonge Street and Highway 11 used to be one and the same, but when the provincial government downloaded roads onto municipalities in the late 1990s, Yonge was no longer officially viewed as one continuous roadway. Technically, Yonge Street is now just the 56 km from inside Toronto's borders to where Highway 11 begins at Barrie. So Yonge may have lost its *Guinness World Records* title as the longest street in the world, but that hasn't stopped Torontonians from continuing to make the claim.

They said it

"Ravines are both a tangible (though often hidden) part of our surroundings and a persistent force in our civic imagination. They are the shared subconscious of the municipality, the places where much of the city's literature is born."

– Robert Fulford in the *National Post*, Aug. 24, 2000

TORONTO BOASTS

- 5,365 km of roads (Edmonton has 1,879 km and Vancouver 1,600 km)
- 7,100 km of sidewalks
- 530 bridges (Vancouver has only 18, Montreal 700)
- 2,007 traffic-control signals and 158,890 streetlights
- 1 million signs
- 55,000-seat Rogers Centre Stadium
- 132 community centres
- North America's largest continuous underground pedestrian system under Toronto's financial core. Known as PATH, it stretches for 27 km and has 1,200 stores and restaurants, five subway stations, Union Station, several entertainment centres and the lower floors of 50 office towers and six major hotels.
- 600 pedestrian crosswalks
- 90 km of bike lanes
- 225 km of biking/hiking trails (Vancouver beats this hands-down with 400 km)

Source: City of Toronto

Did you know...

the official name of the Bloor Street Viaduct—the bridge spanning the Don Valley and connecting Bloor Street and Danforth Avenue—is the Prince Edward Viaduct, but you'll rarely hear it used?

BRANCHING OUT

Though most of its original Carolinian forest was chopped as the city grew, Toronto has a significant second- and later-growth green canopy (17 percent coverage), which it aims to double by 2050.

The city officially owns about half a million trees (the ones that line the streets), and there are another 2.5 million in parks, ravines

The Toronto Islands

The Toronto Islands and the harbour they protect have been important for settlement, commerce, military purposes and general well-being since people first arrived in the area. Not everyone makes the trip today, but going over to "the Island" is still one of the easiest and cheapest ways to get away from it all in the city, and it's only moments from downtown.

Although they loom large in our mental picture of Toronto, the Islands are actually a relatively recent feature on the waterfront. They emerged only a few hundred years ago as eroded material from the Bluffs was deposited east of the Don River by west-flowing lake currents. Over time the sediment gradually created sandbars and marshlands and then a peninsula, which became a haven for waterfowl. In 1792 a 9 km curving landmass was solid enough to be surveyed by the English. Helpfully, a violent storm breached it in 1858. The opening became the harbour's Eastern Gap, and the Islands were well and truly cut off from the mainland.

Aboriginal bands camped in the area in their day and considered it a place of health and relaxation. European settlers took to it in the 1800s. The oldest surviving lighthouse on the Great Lakes was built on Gibraltar Point in 1808-09; its whale-oil lamps guided ships toward Western Gap and kept them from hitting the islands.

Long considered a bucolic place to escape Muddy York, the Islands' first hotel was opened in 1833. In 1862 the Hanlan family settled the Hanlan's Point area, now known for its nude beach.

and natural areas as well as a significant number on private property. In its bid to meet its canopy goal, the city's forestry department offers free trees to homeowners, runs a tree-planting and care program and can subsidize the purchase of larger specimens. Among the 40 species native to the city are basswood, white cedar, black oak, red maple, yellow birch and blue beech.

They, too, built a resort hotel and furthered the Islands' transformation into a recreational destination. Labelled Canada's Coney Island by the 1870s, the western Islands would eventually feature cottages, hotels and businesses, as well as an amusement park and the baseball stadium where Babe Ruth hit his first home run as a professional.

By the late 1800s, Centre Island in particular had became a popular vacation spot for the well-to-do, who built big Victorian summer homes on the waterfront and lagoons close to the Royal Canadian Yacht Club. Seasonal houses and hotels also existed on Ward's and Algonquin Islands, and residents numbered in the thousands by the early 1900s. Some of this was lost when the Island Airport was built (1938-39); more left in the 1950s, when the City of Toronto transferred responsibility for the Islands to the Metro level of government and the modernizing of the islands took place, when homes were torn down to make the setting more park-like. Many residents were not pleased, but today there are still 262 private homes on Ward's and Algonquin Islands, largely a result of fierce opposition from that time.

Today much of the Islands is parkland. Three yacht clubs are located there, and it's a perfect place to rent a bike or boat or go for a stroll. To access the Islands, you cross the harbour by ferry from the foot of Bay Street; more than 1.2 million people make that trip every year.

SPANNING THE DON

The most spectacular bridge in Toronto is the Bloor Viaduct, which joins Bloor Street and Danforth Avenue 40 metres above the Don Valley floor. It's half a kilometre long, 26 metres wide and took four years to construct (1915–19). Showing extraordinary forethought, the builders included a lower deck for trains, long before Toronto's subway system existed. The Toronto Transit Commission (TTC) appropriated

TAKE 5 JACK LAYTON AND OLIVIA CHOW'S
TOP FIVE PLACES TO BIKE IN TORONTO

This husband-and-wife political team of federal NDP leader Jack Layton and MP Olivia Chow is not only a force to be reckoned with in the House of Commons but also on tandem or solo bikes through the streets of Toronto. Both are avid cyclists—Chow has even posted her tips for cycling safety at www.youtube.com/watch?v=FVA8WZ03H8Q—and both served on Toronto city council before heading for Ottawa.

1. **Toronto Islands, from Ward's Island to Hanlan's Point:** There is nothing like the lakeside charm of the Toronto Islands and the numerous viewpoints of the skyline, which is partly why we got married there.

2. **Leslie Street Spit in Tommy Thompson Park:** A perfect trail for bird watchers, and its urban wilderness makes the place very special.

3. **Martin Goodman Trail, starting at the Sunnyside bridge:** Part of the Lake Ontario waterfront trail, it's quite safe and well-marked, which is why it is enjoyed by cyclists, joggers and in-line skaters.

4. **The Don Valley bike path:** This one's like a highway for cyclists, always buzzing with people enjoying the wide variety of urban and natural settings.

5. **Stationary bikes at the U of T's Athletic Centre:** The best place to keep in cycling shape when the weather doesn't permit us to ride on one of the first four trails.

this level when it extended its Bloor line east in 1966.

For many years the Viaduct also attracted people in despair; more than 500 jumped off between 1919 and 2003; a Distress Centre sign still implores those in need to call for help. In 2003 the city finally installed "The Luminous Veil"—a sculpture-like barrier of 9,500 stainless-steel rods designed by architect Dereck Revington—which has effectively ended the bridge's use as a final departure point.

PARK IT!

Toronto has 8,000 hectares of parkland, but what has been forgotten is that it could have been an even grander story. In 1793 the Crown gave the young town about 385 acres near Fort York, at the western entrance to the harbour. Another 81 acres farther east was also set aside for the public. Even better, the two were linked in the early 1820s by a green swath called the "Walks and Gardens."

Because of the loss of life caused by the cholera epidemics of 1832 and 1834, the city was forced to sell the land to raise funds to build a larger hospital. In the 1850s, railroad builders gobbled up what land was left.

The fight to create parkland has been ongoing ever since. The city purchased some land and acquired more through donations and grants from the Crown. In 1857 George W. Allan, a botanist and politician, donated what is now Allan Gardens, on the south side of Carlton Street between Jarvis and Sherbourne streets. The city also gained the Island and Exhibition Park from the Crown in 1867 and 1878, respectively. High Park, one of the most well-loved of today's parks, was donated by John Howard in 1873. Grange Park and Sunnybrook Park also came into the system through donations of land.

More than 100 parks are now scattered throughout the city, covering the gamut from recreational and botanical to heritage and from tiny corner playgrounds to expansive lawns, gardens and forests. Everyone has their favourite. Riverdale Park, divided in two by the DVP, was home to Toronto's original zoo and now hosts a favourite children's destination, Riverdale Farm. Given the turmoil that erupts

They said it

regularly in the provincial legislature, it's ironic that behind the legislature is one of Toronto's quietest downton refuges: Queen's Park, an oval-shaped green space with virtually no recreational facilities, is a forest of leafy coolness in summer.

Given the way the city chewed up farms and undeveloped land through the late 20th century, many now say the jewel in Toronto's crown lies to the east: Rouge Park. At 46.5 sq. km, it's the largest urban park in North America, 13 times larger than New York's Central Park and one of a few areas left in south-central Ontario virtually untouched by development. It's the eastern arm of the historic Carrying Place trail, inspired the work of Group of Seven painter F.H. Varley, and has been the set for a slew of modern-day films.

GOING GREEN

HTO Park is a first step in the ongoing major overhaul and revitalization of Toronto's waterfront. Opened in 2007 and billed as "Toronto's urban beach," the park's centrepiece is a narrow stretch of sand flanking the lake complete with beach umbrellas and chairs. Right at the water's edge is a wooden boardwalk that will eventually link a string of parks and cultural spaces with new urban residential development from the port area to the Humber.

Toronto's green dreams are supported by the provincial Liberal government's own ambitious Greenbelt plan, unveiled in 2005. Encompassing 720,000 hectares (1.8 million acres) of countryside around the Golden Horseshoe, the Greenbelt is designed to keep urban development out of environmentally sensitive land and farmland. It will surround the GTA with green space and prevent urban sprawl, although opponents argue that it will hamper Toronto's growth and strangle the city with unprofitable farms and forests.

PLAY IT AGAIN!

Smoking is not allowed within a 9 m radius of any City of Toronto recreational facility, including any these:

- 66 indoor swimming pools
- 59 outdoor swimming pools
- 113 wading pools
- 68 spray pads
- 11 swimming beaches
- 282 baseball diamonds
- 335 rectangular fields
- 210 tennis court locations (a mix of public and private club facilities)
- 6 skate parks
- 11 cricket clubs
- 5 public golf courses
- 6 curling clubs
- 52 outdoor skating rinks
- 48 indoor skating rinks

Source: City of Toronto

Did you know...

that modern-day efforts to establish a ferry route between Rochester and Toronto have repeatedly failed? The closest surface border crossing for Torontonians heading to the U.S. is at Queenston-Lewiston.

THE TTC BY THE NUMBERS (2008)

- Number of bus routes: 139, with 1,737 buses
- Number of streetcar routes: 11, with 248 streetcars
- Number of subway lines: 3, with about 706 subway cars
- Kilometres operated (bus, streetcar, subway, Rapid Transit): 204,529
- Annual number of passenger trips: 466.7 million
- Highest one-day ridership: 1,686,000 on Oct. 30, 2008
- Revenue passengers (fares collected): $1,485,000
- Fare: $2.75 adult, 70¢ child, $1.85 senior/student
- Number of commuter parking lots: 29
- Number of employees: 11,861

Source: Toronto Transit Commission

TWO SECRET SUBWAY STOPS

They're down there, but you can't use them . . .

1. **Lower Queen:** Built (but not finished) to accommodate an underground streetcar track, this never-used stop below the Queen station at Yonge was abandoned when Torontonians voted to put their money behind the north/south line.

2. **Lower Bay:** Now used mainly for filming ads and movies, Lower Bay was a working station for six months in 1966. It was abandoned when the TTC opted to keep north/south and east/west trains on separate routes instead of linking them. You can catch a glimpse of this station from the front window of a westbound Bloor train just after leaving the Yonge station.

Did you know. . .

that one of the wackiest houses in Toronto is at 473 Clinton St., the home of Albino Carreira? After a 1993 injury, Carreira amused himself by redesigning his mailbox. Today thousands of pool cues and screws—plus some hanging toys and 5,000 lights in the winter—decorate the exterior of his home and garden.

They said it

"I've lived in Forest Hill Village, Riverdale, Summerhill, the Annex and Cabbagetown. Finding the right neighbourhood fit in Toronto is only slightly less tricky than finding the right partner to share it with."

– CBC Radio One's Metro Morning man
Andy Barrie, quoted in the *National Post*

DOWNTOWN

The city's version of what constitutes downtown is that it's from the Don Valley to Bathurst—the lake to Bloor, more or less. To everybody else, downtown is south of Bloor, west of Jarvis and east of University.

Whichever way you look at it, the centre of Toronto is Yonge and Dundas, one of the oldest intersections in the city. Recently transformed, the old crossroads features "concrete park" (Toronto Life Square), the Eaton Centre, the Olympic Spirit building (home of CityTV) and a jumble of small shops, plus flashing electronic billboards. The spot is so busy that a "scramble" intersection was introduced in 2008; on foot you can now cross the street on the diagonal.

Downtown includes the financial district, law courts and offices, the Ontario legislature, several hospitals, three universities and a huge range of retail outlets and places to eat, drink and be merry.

It is largely a safe, easy and entertaining place to live and work, which is why its residential numbers are going up. The downtown population grew by 65 percent over the last 30 years; between 2001 and 2006 alone, 14,800 new residents moved in, a 10 percent increase. The influx is largely young (under 40), well-educated, child-free singles and couples. A glut of new condos and high-rises is attempting to meet the demand for living quarters, thus increasing the downtown population density, especially along the waterfront. Almost one-third of new downtown developments since 2001 have 30 or more storeys.

Weather

Toronto has what climatologists describe as a humid continental climate, which means it experiences warm humid summers and cold winters. Torontonians consider it a birthright to complain endlessly in winter about snowstorms and bitterly cold winds, then gripe about the humidity and heat of summer. The truth is that Toronto's climate is among the milder and more pleasant of all cities in Canada.

Toronto is on the same latitude as Cannes and Boston, and this southerly location (for Canada) helps moderate the effects of winter. When it does show up, however, winter can bring major snowfalls—often the result of powerful storms that come from "Colorado Lows," which pick up moisture as they cross Lake Ontario. Extended snow-free periods can occur even in mid-winter, but significant snow can also show up as late as April. Anybody who has lived in Toronto knows and fears a cold snap—a period of days, or even a week to two weeks, when temperatures drop to -10°C and often feel much colder because of north winds. Chilly winter days usually alternate with mild ones, with interludes of 5° to 10°C or even higher.

Toronto's climate is also influenced by its location on the shores of Lake Ontario. Proximity to all of that water ensures that the city is warmer in winter and cooler in summer than places farther inland, and it's also the reason behind Toronto's summer humidity.

Spring is usually beautiful, and flowering can begin in April.

TAKE 5 TORONTO'S TOP FIVE
RECORD HOT TEMPERATURES

1. **40.6°C**, recorded July 8, 1936
2. **39°C**, recorded Aug. 13, 1918
3. **38°C**, recorded Sept. 2, 1953
4. **37°C**, recorded June 30, 1964
5. **34°C**, recorded May 18, 1962

Source: Environment Canada

Summer does include periods of scorching weather, some of it with oppressive humidity. But the best season of all, many would say, is autumn, when Toronto's extensive tree canopy makes a glorious spectacle all over the city.

AVERAGE DAILY TEMPERATURES (°C)

Jan	Feb	Mar	Apr	May	Jun	Jul	Aug	Sep	Oct	Nov	Dec
-6.3	-5.4	-0.4	6.3	12.9	17.	20.8	19.9	15.3	8.9	3.2	-2.9

Source: Environment Canada

AND THE WINNER IS . . .

- Record high: 40.6°C, recorded July 8, 1936
- Record low: -33°C, recorded Jan. 10, 1859
- Record rainfall in one day: 121.4 mm, recorded Oct. 15, 1954
- Record snowfall in one day: 48.3 cm, recorded Dec. 11, 1944
- Record wind speed: 97 km/h, recorded March 15, 1959
- Record wind gust: 135 km/h, recorded July 1, 1956
- Record wind chill: -36.6°C, recorded Jan. 24, 1963
- Record humidex: 44.5°C, recorded June 18, 1957
- Record hours of sunshine: 14.6, recorded June 26, 1999
- Record number of smog advisories: 48, recorded in 2005

Source: Environment Canada

TAKE 5 TORONTO'S TOP FIVE
RECORD HUMIDEX TEMPERATURES

1. **44.5°C**, recorded June 18, 1957
2. **44°C**, recorded Sept. 2, 1953
3. **43°C**, recorded July 28, 1964
4. **42°C**, recorded Aug. 1, 1955
5. **40°C**, recorded May 29, 1969

Source: Environment Canada

FEELING HOT, HOT, HOT

Toronto ranks ninth out of 100 Canadian centres when it comes to the hottest summers. The highest average afternoon temperature is 25°C in June, July and August, about the same as in Ottawa, Saskatoon and Fredericton. Two British Columbia communities on the same list claim the summer extremes: Kamloops is the nation's hottest place (with an average temperature of 27°C) and Prince Rupert the chilliest (16°C). Other provincial capitals on the list include Winnipeg (No. 27), Quebec City (No. 45) and Halifax (No. 88).

Source: Environment Canada

HERE COMES THE SUN

Toronto just makes it into the top third of sunniest Canadian cities, in a list of 100. Its average of 2,038 hours of sunshine a year places it in 33rd position. The Prairie provinces are Canada's sunniest region: Medicine Hat captures the No. 1 spot with 2,513 hours of sunshine yearly, and Calgary, Regina, Edmonton, Moose Jaw and Winnipeg are among the top 12. Toronto is just ahead of Whitehorse (1,855 hours) and way ahead of Kingston (No. 44), Moncton (No. 63) and Vancouver (No. 76). Prince Rupert, B.C., has the least sunshine yearly by a wide margin, only about 1,229 hours, or 60 percent of the Toronto average.

Source: Environment Canada

HUMIDITY

Compared to areas to the south, prolonged high humidity is unusual in Canada; generally, the humidex decreases with increasing latitude. Toronto is an exception to this rule, not only because of its proximity to

TAKE 5 DAVID PHILLIPS'S TOP FIVE
TORONTO WEATHER EXTREMES

David Phillips is Environment Canada's senior climatologist, an author and a national weather personality. A spokesperson for the Meteorological Service of Canada, he is also the man behind the popular *Weather Trivia Calendar*. He claims that Canada has been "blessed with one of the world's healthiest and safest climates."

1. **Hottest temperature (40.6°C on July 8, 1936):** Canada's longest and widest-felt heat wave was devastating for Torontonians. Horses pulling milk and bread wagons dropped dead in the streets, and most retail stores, apart from those with air conditioning, were empty; laundry and store clerks collapsed from the heat. Ice cream sales skyrocketed, and ice deliveries rose 80 percent and were permitted on Sundays. In total, 225 Torontonians died.

2. **Coldest recent temperature (-31.3°C on Jan. 4, 1981, at Pearson Airport):** Thousands of people were trapped in the subway as trains literally froze in their tracks; 16 passengers fainted in the crush. Thousands more were late for work because cars wouldn't start. Harbour police boats were trapped by thick ice, and the flow of natural gas slowed. It was also too cold for crime; the police reported quiet times and no arrests.

Lake Ontario but also because moist warm air from the Gulf of Mexico and the Caribbean can reach the city, bringing humidex values close to 45°C. This makes Toronto the 15th most humid summer city in the country (out of 82), according to Environment Canada. Windsor ranks No. 1, followed by Sarnia, Kingston and Hamilton, all in Ontario.

3. **Snowiest day (48.3 cm on Dec. 11, 1944):** This blizzard shut down Toronto with the greatest single-day snowfall in the city's history: the two-day dump left 57.2 cm in total. The armed forces cleared streets and sidewalks. All traffic except for emergency vehicles were banned from streets, although trucks replaced ambulances to take expectant mothers and the sick to hospital. Home deliveries of milk, ice and fuel were cancelled and funerals postponed.

4. **Lowest air pressure (96.2 kPa on Jan. 26, 1978):** When a huge winter storm pounded southern Ontario, air pressure in Toronto reached a record low. Combined with wind gusts over 115 km/h, this popped out skyscraper windows and littered the downtown area with glass. Winds were so fierce they blew pedestrians off their feet, and downtown became a ghost town. The water level rose and overflowed the shoreline, turning the Lakeshore into a mammoth skating rink.

5. **Rainiest day (121.4 mm on Oct. 15, 1954):** Hurricane Hazel drenched an already soggy city with an estimated 300 million tonnes of rain. The storm left a nightmare of destruction in and around Toronto: lost streets, washed-out bridges and untold personal tragedy.

TAKE 5 FIVE WAYS TO SAY
"HOLY $!!$, IT'S COLD!"

1. **Chinese:** "hladno je!"
2. **Italian:** "E molto freddo!"
3. **Punjabi:** "aus hY hl srdl"
4. **Spanish:** "Hace mucho frio!"
5. **Portuguese:** "Esta muito frio!"

SMOG

Smog is an oppressive plague of Toronto summers. Intense heat episodes often feature both high humidity and dangerous levels of airborne smog. Worse, summer smog has steadily increased in recent years, caused mainly by locally produced vehicle exhaust and air pollution from heavy industry in the Midwestern United States and southern Ontario. Toronto Public Health estimates that 1,700 Toronto residents die prematurely every year as a result of air pollution, while another 6,000 are admitted to hospitals because of complications from it.

When the Air Quality Index reaches or exceeds 50, the Ontario Ministry of Environment and the City of Toronto issue smog alerts. The City's Air Quality Information Line provides up-to-date information on the smog-alert status. The summer of 2005 currently holds the record for smog warnings in the city, at 48 days.

GROWING SEASON

Toronto is a great place for gardeners. Most years the area has about 138 frost-free days, starting around April 29 and ending around Oct.

Did you know. . .

that the first official weather observation in Canada was taken in Toronto in 1839?

TAKE 5 TORONTO'S FIVE
RAINIEST DAYS

1. **121.4 mm,** recorded Oct. 15, 1954
2. **118.5 mm,** recorded July 28, 1980
3. **108 mm,** recorded Sept. 8, 1948
4. **92.7 mm,** recorded May 31, 1944
5. **86.1 mm,** recorded Nov. 10, 1962

Source: Environment Canada

15. In addition, good soil, the availability of clean water and the moderating effects of Lake Ontario help make it an excellent place for growing a range of produce.

Over the past 10 years, the number of community garden sites in the city has grown to more than 100; pilot projects in commercial agriculture include rooftop herb and vegetable gardens. Toronto boasts 27 farmers' markets that feature local bounty; they're usually open between May and October, although six operate year-round.

PRECIPITATION

- Total annual precipitation: 793 mm
- Annual rainfall: 685 mm
- Annual snowfall: 115 cm
- Percentage of precipitation that falls as snow: 14.55

Source: Environment Canada

IT'S RAINING, IT'S POURING

Toronto's average of 793 mm of annual precipitation puts it among the least wet of the 100 most populated cities and towns in Canada. It takes the 69th spot; Prince Rupert, B.C., tops the list with 2,594 mm a year. The city ranks 66th for "highest number of wet days" and 58th for the "highest number of very wet days" (more than 25 mm precipitation in a day).

Source: Environment Canada

CH-CH-CHILLY

Toronto is known for mild winters punctuated by dramatic exceptions to the rule. It ranks 72nd out of 100 Canadian centres on Environment Canada's "coldest winter" list. The lowest average nighttime temperature in December, January and February is -8°C, about the same as Corner

Storm of the Century

Hurricane Hazel began to gain speed about 80 km east of Grenada; as it tracked northward, it left a trail of destruction that would mark it as one of the worst natural disasters of the century. In Garden City, South Carolina, it left only two of 275 homes standing. By 9 p.m. on Oct. 14, 1954, it was over Rochester and Buffalo and headed for Toronto. Most forecasters predicted it would weaken, but instead gained in intensity.

The city had already received above-average rainfall in the preceding month, so when Hazel pounded it with 124 km/h winds and a record rainfall of 285 millimetres over 48 hours, the rain simply ran off the surface of the saturated ground into rivers and creeks, filling them to capacity and beyond, raising some by 8 metres. Throughout the city, 20 bridges were swept away or damaged beyond repair. Trains were derailed; roads were washed out. Overflowing rivers tore houses from their foundations and picked up cars and mobile homes.

In the Humber River Valley, Raymore Drive was demolished and 35 people were killed. Five firemen who were sent to rescue people trapped in a car were also killed. The Holland Marsh north of the city became a lake, and rainfall destroyed houses and crops and forced residents to flee.

In total, 81 people were killed in Toronto and thousands were left homeless. Total cost of the destruction was estimated at $100 million (about $1 billion today). As a result of the disaster, and to ensure the loss of life from such events never happened again, conservation authorities were granted powers to buy and regulate floodplain land and to create flood-control and flood-warning systems.

They said it

"Twenty-three cruisers here at the Humber. The life-saving people say not to launch a boat of any size...repeat, of any size...in this river. Nothing can make it. Anyone in it will be killed for sure."
– A police radio message describing the futility of launching boats into the river during Hurricane Hazel.

Brook and Hamilton. Cities substantially colder than Toronto include Fredericton (-14°C), Sudbury (-16°C), Ont., and Winnipeg (-21°C). Yellowknife is the No. 1 cold spot (-29°C) in the country.

Source: Environment Canada

WHEN IT FEELS WORSE THAN IT IS

The colder months are also the windier months in Toronto, and most of the strongest winds (faster than 52 km/h) blow then. Wind chill becomes a daily topic of conversation and a standard item in forecasts. Typically, the wind will make it feel colder than -20°C on 27.5 days in a year, and 3.7 of these feel colder than -30°C.

It has never seemed colder in Toronto than on Jan. 4, 1981, when the wind-chill factor made it feel like -44°C. The coldest it has ever been in Canada was -64°C, which earned the folks in Yellowknife the unfortunate bragging rights.

Did you know...

that every year at winter's kickoff, typically in mid-November, Toronto Police Services and OPP deal with about a thousand fender-benders in the city?

Did you know...

that water consumption levels in Toronto reached record levels (182 million gallons) on Sept. 2, 1952, during a record-breaking heat wave?

SKYLINE WEATHER FORECASTS

A unique public-weather beacon has been telling Torontonians the forecast since 1951. Topping the Canada Life building at the corner of University Avenue and Queen Street, it uses 1,560 light bulbs to com-

Call in the Troops

Early in 1999, a series of record snowstorms disrupted the life of Canada's largest metropolis. More than five million people were affected and 11 people died.

The first and worst storm arrived on Jan. 2, dumping between 20 and 40 cm of snow on the city. Thousands of people spent one of the busiest travel days of the year stranded at Toronto's Pearson International Airport. Four more storms followed in quick succession, dropping a record 118 cm of snow in 12 days—4 cm more than the annual average for the city and the snowiest two-week period since 1871.

With no end in sight, on Jan. 13 then Mayor Mel Lastman asked for military help. More than 400 troops from CFB Petawawa and other regions of Ontario and Quebec descended on the crippled city. Headed by Lt.-Col. Julian Chapman of the Toronto Scottish Regiment, the soldiers transformed their 14-tonne Bisons (eight-wheeled armoured vehicles) into on-site emergency rooms and ambulances, transported patients from accident scenes to hospitals and cleared inaccessible streets. Most troops broke camp Jan. 17, while 120 stayed to help with snow removal.

Lastman's request was mocked by comedians and Toronto bashers across the country. While some Torontonians were embarrassed by the mayor's decision, many more applauded his initiative for getting the city moving again. Not only did the snowstorm bring the city to a standstill but it was also extremely expensive to clear. Toronto usually spends about $65 million annually on snow removal; by the end of January 1999, the snowy chaos had cost the city $70 million.

TAKE 5 FIVE AVERAGE DECEMBER
TEMPERATURES AT 43°N

Toronto sits at 43°40' N on the shore of Lake Ontario and has an average December temperature of -2.9°C. Here's how five cities at the same latitude around the globe fare in December:

1. **Sapporo, Japan** (43°05' N): -3°C
2. **Vladivostok, Russia** (43°09' N): -10°C
3. **Nice, France** (43°42' N): 10°C
4. **Portland, Maine** (43°40' N): -3°C
5. **Sioux Falls, South Dakota** (43°33' N): -27°C

Source: Environment Canada

municate weather trends. The colour of the lights and the way they light up are the keys to interpreting the forecast:

- green means fair weather
- red means cloudy
- flashing red means rain
- flashing white means snow

If the bulbs light from the bottom of the beacon upward, the forecast is for rising temperatures. If they light in the other direction, temperatures will fall. If they remain steady, that's what the temperature is expected to do. The forecasts, which come from the Ontario Weather Centre, are updated four times a day. For decades the *Globe and Mail* used the beacon as an icon on its weather page.

Did you know...

that in 2006, the number of smog-advisory days dropped dramatically to 11 from 48 in 2005—the lowest annual total since 2000? This was largely due to regular rains and citizens' conservation efforts.

PASS THE SHOVEL

Despite sometimes spectacular dumps of the white stuff, Toronto ranks only 79th out of 100 Canadian centres in total annual snowfall. Its annual average is 115 cm, well behind the Newfoundland centres that claim first and second spots: Gander (443 cm) and Corner Brook (422 cm).

Because of Toronto's close proximity to the Great Lakes, it is subject to whiteouts and lake-effect snow each winter during typical westerly or northwesterly winds. Rare easterlies and southeasterlies can also generate snow squalls from Lake Ontario.

Source: Environment Canada

TAKE 5 FIVE FAVOURITE
TORONTO WINTER ACTIVITIES

1. **Santa Claus Parade:** Toronto's Christmas parade in mid-November attracts more than 500,000 viewers to the streets, and millions more watch the TV broadcast. Established in 1905, it's the world's largest parade and the longest-running children's parade across the globe.

2. **First Night Toronto:** This alcohol-free winter event is aimed at families and provides a cultural alternative to New Year's Eve revelry. Held at the Rogers Centre, it features a wide variety of artists and art forms.

3. **Skating at City Hall:** A few turns around the rink at Nathan Phillips Square is a quintessential winter experience. The skating is free but weather dependent; the natural ice requires sub-zero temperatures.

4. **Cavalcade of Lights:** From the last weekend in November to the end of December, Nathan Phillips Square is also the hub for an outdoor celebration that includes concerts, fireworks, Saturday-night skates to live music, a fair trade market and a brightly lit tree and square.

5. **Tobogganing:** Free sledding destinations in the city include High Park and the Don Valley ravine. If you prefer the quiet and slower pace of snowshoes, try Queens Park or the Centreville Amusement Park.

TAKE 5 FIVE WEIRD
TORONTO WEATHER FACTS

1. Toronto has generally received its biggest snowfalls on Thursdays.
2. Over the past 170 years, it has always snowed in Toronto after the first day of spring.
3. Small frogs rained on downtown Toronto during a heavy rainstorm on June 9, 1884.
4. Toronto gets more lightning flashes in an average year (11,136) than any other city in Canada.
5. Fifteen percent of Toronto's annual precipitation falls as snow (the Canadian average is 39 percent).

Source: David Phillips

WHITE CHRISTMAS

According to Environment Canada, Toronto has a 57 percent chance of a white Christmas (in the 1980s, the likelihood was slightly higher). Snow does fall in Toronto before Christmas, but most of it appears after the New Year, usually from mid-January to March. Canadian cities almost guaranteed to have a blanket of the white stuff on Dec. 25 include Goose Bay, N.L. (100 percent), Winnipeg (98 percent) and Charlottetown (87 percent).

Snow in the air and at least two centimetres on the ground is considered the "perfect" white Christmas. These specific conditions are likely to occur in Toronto only 13 percent of Christmases.

Did you know...

that in Toronto, lightning hits about two times per square kilometre annually?

PAYING FOR WINTER

Removing and disposing of the roughly 115 cm of snow that falls on Toronto every year is essential to keeping the city moving, particularly after a major dump. More than 530 city employees are involved in snow removal, augmented by an additional 1,068 workers from private firms.

- Total centerline* roads: 5,600 km
- Expressways: 133 km
- Main roads (arterials): 1,095 km
- Collector roads: 889 km
- Local roads: 3,163 km
- Laneways: 320 km
- Number of streets: 9,500
- Total sidewalks: 7,945 km
- Plowed sidewalks: 6,000 km
- Total number of opened driveways (which allow vehicles to pass after the snowplow has gone by): 262,000
- Annual truckloads of snow disposed of: 40,000
- Number of disposal sites: 9 (These include a stationary melter in the parking lot of Ontario Place; during times of heavy accumulation, snow is dumped here to melt gradually in warmer weather. Snow is not dumped in Lake Ontario.)
- Number of vehicles in the snow-removal fleet: 1,096
- 2008 budget for snow removal: $62.8 million

* *"centerline km" measures road length; "lane km" would be what is actually plowed: centerline km multiplied by the number of lanes on the road.*

Did you know. . .

that Toronto uses 136,000 tonnes of salt to de-ice its streets and sidewalks in an average year, based on a 10-year average? This is more than four times the road salt Calgary uses each year, which comes in at 30,000 to 40,000 tonnes.

DROUGHT

According to Environment Canada Toronto is the country's 32nd driest city, although it ranks 35th in "most dry days."

Excessive heat is a stressor in Toronto. The summer of 2007 was the most arid summer in 50 years, reporting 95 consecutive days without significant rain. This period demonstrated the potential impact of extremely dry summers in the city. Most trees went thirsty that year, making them vulnerable to high winds, pests and disease.

TAKE5 LAWSON OATES' TOP FIVE REASONS WHY T.O. IS AN INTERESTING PLACE TO WATCH WEATHER

Lawson Oates, the director of the Toronto Environment Office, has lived in Toronto since 1961. His interest and concern over climate change was sparked during his graduate studies in the 1980s at York University's Faculty of Environmental Studies. He leads a team of environmentalists working to encourage all Torontonians to help combat climate change.

1. **Variety:** The city experiences widely varied weather patterns and consequences.
2. **It's hard to predict:** Low-pressure cells passing either north or south of the city by just a little can create widely differing weather.
3. **Lake Ontario:** Toronto would have an extreme continental climate were it not for the moderating effects of the Great Lakes in general and Lake Ontario in particular.
4. **Climate change:** Mark Twain said, "Climate is what we expect, but weather is what we get." These days "what we can expect" is changing.
5. **Weather affects everything we do:** Weather is integral to our lives and our livelihoods and provides endless reasons for Torontonians to complain.

WIND

Standing at the corner of King and Bay streets—arguably Toronto's windiest downtown corner—you might not think that the city is only the 32nd windiest in the country. Although the average wind speed is 15 km/hr, some areas can be exceptionally breezy. The tall buildings on Bay Street, for example, can funnel wind up from the harbour with breathtaking force. St. John's is the country's windiest city (average speed 23 km/hr), and Kelowna, B.C., has the most placid breezes (5 km/hr). Toronto is less windy than nearby Hamilton, which ranks 11th in the country, experiencing winds similar in force to Regina, Montreal, Charlottetown and Corner Brook.

Source: Environment Canada

STORM DAMAGE

Just over 50 years after Hurricane Hazel devastated Toronto, a second storm described as a "one in a thousand years" occurrence swept through the city on Aug. 19, 2005. In less than two hours, up to 183 mm of rain fell in parts of the northern end of Toronto, and roads and bridges were washed out. Insurance claims for backed-up sewers and flood damage exceeded $500 million, which equalled 50 percent of all payoffs for sewer backups in the province during the previous decade. The normally tame Black Creek created a hole 7 m deep in Finch Avenue West, severing the road. Reconstruction took six months. It is now almost impossible to get basement flood insurance in flood-prone parts of Toronto.

THE SKY IS FALLING

During a wild March storm in 2007, sheets of ice—some 2 cm thick and as big as tabletops—blew off the CN Tower and other buildings in the heart of downtown Toronto. Experts said it was the first and (so far) only time in the CN Tower's history that ice had built up in that way or posed a threat to public safety.

Winds gusting to 65 km/h had smeared a wet snow-rain mixture across the Tower's walls, which adhered in a flash freeze. The unexpected occurred when direct sunlight began melting the ice next to the concrete, allowing higher winds to lift chunks of ice away from the wall.

The chunks fell at speeds up to 360 km/h onto the Gardiner Expressway and on streets below, as far as King Street, cracking windshields, denting car roofs and making walking hazardous. One downtown hotel even supplied guests with hardhats. Police closed some streets surrounding the tower. No injuries were reported, and most pedestrians seemed unfazed.

A WIND-POWER FIRST

In 1999 the Toronto Renewable Energy Cooperative formed WindShare, a joint venture with Toronto Hydro Energy Services, to develop the first North American utility-scale wind turbine in an urban environment. Completed in 2003, the $1.8-million turbine sits near the Dufferin Gate at Exhibition Place; it generates an average of 1,000 megawatt hours of power annually, equivalent to the electricity needs of more than 200 homes. It also displaces up to 380 tonnes of carbon dioxide annually—the same as taking 1,300 cars off the road or planting 30,000 trees a year.

The 30-storey turbine, likened by some to a giant beanstalk, is roughly one-seventh the height of the CN Tower and clearly visible to the thousands of commuters who use Lakeshore Boulevard and the Gardiner Expressway. Many green Torontonians see the structure as a symbolic tribute to the Kyoto Protocol on global warming, and even as a physical rebuttal (a finger in the sky) to those who insist that implementing Kyoto would devastate Canada's economy.

Did you know. . .

that Toronto's Urban Forestry Services' tree-planting program now includes species that are more tolerant of heat, drought and pests?

GREEN CHANGE IS IN THE AIR

At a special meeting of Toronto's Parks and Environment Committee in January of 2008, six climate-change adaptation experts agreed that if Toronto didn't change its ways, it would face serious climate-change challenges: more frequent and severe weather events; extreme heat; urban flooding; drought; and new and invasive species. They called for action to protect human health, the environment and the economy.

As a result, Toronto is taking serious steps to reduce its ecological footprint. The city has spent more than $80 million in energy retrofits in buildings and another $30 million in energy-related projects in city facilities. It passed an anti-idling bylaw and implemented a policy to reduce emissions on smog-alert days.

The city also offers financial rewards for community-based environmental projects, such as renewable-energy initiatives, local food production and green roofs. Its green-bin initiative, which aims to divert waste from landfills by turning organic material into compost, is being phased in to more than 4,500 apartment buildings, condominiums and co-ops.

Toronto has also begun a major overhaul of its transit system to try to reduce reliance on cars. Currently, drivers make more than 100,000 trips into downtown Toronto every morning, and the numbers are predicted to rise. It is hoped that the Toronto Transit Commission's City Light Rail Plan to extend mass-transit lines will help change transit and transportation thinking, revitalize neighbourhoods, spur economic growth and help clean the air.

Weblinks

Weather, or Not
www.weatheroffice.gc.ca/city/pages/on-143_metric_e.html
Canada's weather office provides Toronto with current weather conditions and a seven-day forecast.

Cough, Gasp
www.airqualityontario.com/alerts/alert.cfm
Up-to-date information on air quality across the province by city (and in Toronto's case, by area of the city) from the Ontario Ministry of the Environment. Also, news and information about climate challenges facing Ontario and, by extension, its biggest city.

Avoiding Gridlock
www.canada.com/cityguides/toronto/traffic/toronto_central.html
Twenty cameras on the 401 and the Don Valley Parkway provide an instant look at both traffic and weather conditions across the city.

Culture

Reduced to painting commercial portraits, internationally renowned modern artist and author Wyndham Lewis bitterly described 1940s Toronto as a "hell of dullness."

It's a whole other story today. The city is a cosmopolitan artist-friendly town undergoing a major cultural renaissance. This is nowhere more evident than in architecture, where the *modus operandi* of the last five years has been redesign. There's the Art Gallery of Ontario and Royal Ontario Museum, both updated by world-renowned "starchitects" Frank Gehry and Daniel Libeskind, respectively. And then there's the funky redesign of the once staid Ontario College of Art main campus by avant-garde British architect Will Alsop, featuring multi-coloured giant "crayons" as support columns.

Toronto has also nurtured and been home to such Canadian literary leading lights as Margaret Atwood, Barry Callaghan, Austin Clarke, Michael Ondaatje and Nino Ricci, to name a few. It's also Canada's publishing centre; McLelland & Stewart, Coach House and Anansi Press are among the many publishers that collectively account for more than 70 percent of all national book-publishing revenues.

Toronto is an incubator for film stars such as Sarah Polley and Mike Myers and home to directors such as Norman Jewison, Atom Egoyan and David Cronenberg. The Toronto International Film Festival

(TIFF), one of the world's most prestigious, has a knack for premiering popular hits, such as the Oscar-sweeping *Slumdog Millionaire*. It's no surprise—Toronto is North America's third-largest film-and-TV production centre, providing 30 percent of Canada's jobs in the motion-picture and sound-recording industries.

And with 90-plus live-theatre venues, including the Princess of

Genius

If a buoyant economy can be said to raise all ships, so too does the presence of genius raise the stock of a place in the minds of its citizens. Glenn Gould's musical genius most likely would have been realized elsewhere, but the fact that it was made manifest in Toronto, nurtured by homegrown institutions and the city's landscapes, gave both the city and its people a tremendous boost in confidence. Future genius-artists who see Toronto as their home and the world as their stage will be Gould's progeny.

Gould began studying at the Toronto Conservatory of Music, was inspired by the age of seven by the concerts of the Toronto Symphony, won prizes in the local Kiwanis Music Festival, played his first piano concert at the Canadian National Exhibition and first appeared on radio on CFRB. He graduated from Malvern Collegiate Institute and the University of Toronto and later played on stage at Massey Hall, the Art Gallery of Toronto and the Eaton and Metropolitan auditoriums. In turn, the CBC and the city nurtured his recording career and provided him with the artistic outlets he needed.

Gould was always convinced of his genius, but when Columbia Records launched *The Goldberg Variations* in 1956 when he was just 24, it made him an international superstar and put him in demand around the world. The question on everyone's lips was, "Who is this unusual creature from the hinterland?"

Wales Theatre and the Royal Alexandra Theatre, Toronto is the third-largest English-speaking theatre centre in the world, behind London and New York. In addition, it's also home to the National Ballet of Canada and more than fifty other dance companies, the Canadian Opera Company and the Toronto Symphony Orchestra. Torontonians love music, and the artists and bands incubated in its clubs and record-

The answer was "one of the most important piano virtuosos of the 20th century." As an artist, Gould was devoted to music and married to originality. He developed a singular style of playing, with his back hunched and his head held horizontal to the keyboard. To watch him in concert was to see Bach or Schoenberg brought to life, their rhythmic expression as clearly moving through his body and fingers as through the steel strings of his concert grand.

In 1964, despite increasing demand, Gould stopped performing live, choosing instead to devote his energies to writing and recording. At the CBC he began to explore the electronic media, truly putting him ahead of his time.

Throughout his career, Torontonians remained endlessly curious. Gould fought for his privacy, and most people had to satisfy themselves with his televised appearances or an occasional sighting at a Fran's Diner.

Gould died in 1984, much too young at age 50. The public paid its respect at St. Paul's Cathedral; his estate was left to the Toronto Humane Society and the Salvation Army. He lies at rest beside his mother in Mount Pleasant Cemetery. A statue of him sits outside CBC Headquarters on Front Street: on a park bench, in his trademark winter coat, which he often wore even in the heat of summer.

ing studios are legion—from Sharon, Lois and Bram to Rush and from Moe Koffman and Glenn Gould to Robbie Robertson.

In Toronto culture is not an adornment, it's an industry. English-speaking Canadians come to the city to "make it." Although the talent drain to New York City and Los Angeles still occurs, increasingly Canadians and Torontonians make exceptional livings across a broad spectrum of art endeavours right here at home.

If Wyndham Lewis were alive today, he would be pleasantly surprised—and never bored.

TAKE 5 FIVE LEGENDARY TORONTO MUSIC VENUES

1. **Massey Hall:** The first concert at Massey Hall was held in 1894 and showcased Handel's *Messiah*. Since then the stately hall, with a seating capacity of 2,753, has hosted operas, symphonies, jazz concerts, musicals, beauty pageants, and boxing and wrestling matches.

2. **The Riverboat:** This small 100-seat club in what is now upscale Yorkville opened in 1964 and was the most famous coffeehouse in Canada, featuring such musicians as Bruce Cockburn, Gordon Lightfoot, Murray McLauchlan and Joni Mitchell. It closed in 1979.

3. **Roy Thomson Hall:** The 2,630-seat home of the Toronto Symphony Orchestra opened in 1982.

4. **Horseshoe Tavern:** In its early days after it opened in 1947, the club was a restaurant with live music featuring country artists. Then it was new wave/punk acts; then it was practically anything. Stompin' Tom Connors once played there 25 nights in a row.

5. **The Rivoli:** Since its 1982 opening, this Queen Street West club has presented both music and comedy along with delicious food. According to legend, *Saturday Night Live*'s Mike Myers modelled his character "Dieter" after a black-clad Rivoli waiter.

ARTISTS

- Number of artists in Toronto: 21,025, about twice as many as Montreal
- Number of artists in Canada: 130,700
- Toronto artists' average earnings: $34,100
- Gap between Toronto artists' earnings and overall workforce average: 11 percent
- Gap between Canadian artists' earnings and overall workforce average: 26 percent

About 1.6 percent of Torontonians classify themselves as artists, giving the city the fifth-highest ranking in the country behind Vancouver, Victoria, Montreal and North Van. That said, three of Toronto's neighbourhoods have the highest concentration of artists in Canada:

- The Annex, from Bloor to Dupont, has 845 artists out of 15,590 workers, a 5.4 percent concentration that is seven times the national average.
- Queen Street West has a 5.2 percent concentration of artists and plays a big part in T.O.'s independent-music scene.
- Little Italy, at College west of Bathurst, is an up-and-coming growth area for artists; 5.1 percent of its residents work in the arts.

Source: Canada Council

Did you know...

that the buskers in the TTC subway stations are all licensed by the city? There's an annual audition for wannabe performers; if you make the grade you can ply your trade if you display your licence (the fee is $25).

BOHEMIAN INDEX

The "bohemian index" refers to the size of the creative community. Canada as a whole has an average 6.1 creative types per 1,000 people. Here's how some of the nation's largest cities measured up.

- Vancouver: 9.8
- Toronto: 9.4
- Victoria: 8.8
- Montreal: 8.2
- Hamilton: 5.3
- Windsor: 3.7
- Sudbury: 3

Source: Investing In Children

TORONTO HAS . . .

- 2,740 actors
- 1,280 artisans and craftspeople
- 405 conductors, composers and arrangers
- 755 dancers
- 3,995 musicians and singers
- 1,890 painters, sculptors and other visual artists
- 5,120 producers, directors and choreographers
- 4,265 writers

Source: Canada Council

ALL IN A YEAR'S WORK

On average, artists in Toronto earn $34,100 a year, the highest in the country for arts-related workers:

Did you know. . .

that the rotunda of the old Don Jail was used as the set for the New York nightclub where Tom Cruise's character worked in the 1988 move *Cocktail*?

TAKE 5 DAVE BIDINI'S FIVE
FAVOURITE SONGS ABOUT TORONTO

Born and raised in the Toronto suburb of Etobicoke, Dave Bidini is a musician, writer, founder of the rock band Rheostatics (11 albums since 1987) and a sports lover, particularly hockey. His writing credits include the books *Baseballissimo* and *Tropic of Hockey* (and its film adaptation).

1. **"CN Tower," Michael Jordana and the Poles.** Toronto New Wave is forever under-appreciated by Canadian rock historians, and this song was its apotheosis.

2. **"Toronto Tontos," Max Webster.** Both punk and prog, New Wave and hard rock, this tribute to Yonge Street denim draggers features whirlies, Mexican lyrics, "free publicity's not free when it's public," a guitar solo to crumble cement and very loud drumming.

3. **"Bobcaygeon," Tragically Hip.** Cottage country to city and back again. Late summer, when the city empties, and you're alone in a big place. Woolen-sweater pop. Upper Canadian.

4. **"Alberta Bound," Gordon Lightfoot.** Buddy's in the city and having a crummy time, dreaming of home: "It's snowing in the city and the streets are dark and gritty." Before patios and nightclub shootings, evoking a tavern-town, Prairie immigrants drawn like moths to a lamp.

5. **"Shady Street," The Lawn.** Another grossly neglected but hugely influential (to me, anyway) band. A leafy town, always a surprise to Vancouverites, parks and play, baseball, smokes on a park bench, a million languages.

Occupation	Toronto	Canada
Writers	$36,527	$31,911
Producers, directors and choreographers	$49,429	$43,111
Actors	$26,343	$21,597
Artisans	$20,084	$15,533
Painters and sculptors	$40,023	$18,156
Dancers	$18,542	$14,587
Musicians and singers	$23,894	$16,090

Source: Canada Council

THAT'S AN ORDER

- Toronto recipients of the Order of Canada   799
- Toronto Members of the Order   424
- Toronto Officers of the Order   283
- Toronto Companions of the Order   92

Source: Office of the Governor General of Canada

RECOGNITION OF THE ARTS

Artists and arts organizations in Toronto get a sizeable chunk of Canada Council funding. In 2007–08 the total was $34.6 million, about two-thirds of the support the Council directed to Ontario. Some of the major recipients were the Canadian Opera Company, the National Ballet of Canada, the Toronto Symphony Orchestra and the Canadian Stage Company.

Did you know...

that Canadian singer/songwriting legend Neil Young and funkster Rick James played together in the same Toronto band? The Mynah Birds performed in local clubs during the mid-1960s, before Young hit it big in folk-rock and James made a splash with "Superfreak."

TAKE *5* AMY HARRIS' FIVE ICONIC
BUT OBSCURE NOVELS ABOUT TORONTO

Amy Lavender Harris is the author of *Imagining Toronto* (Mansfield Press, 2009). The curator of a large private library of books set in Toronto, she is the city's go-to source for everything about its literary heritage.

1. **Noman's Land** by Gwendolyn MacEwen (Coach House, 1985). In this episodic novel by the Governor General Award-winning poet, an amnesic emerges lost and naked in the Ontario wilderness and hitch-hikes to Toronto to search for his memory. Realizing that Toronto also suffers from identity problems, Noman crafts a mythology for the city—and an identity for himself—out of iconic places and events from history.

2. **The Meeting Point** by Austin Clarke (Macmillan, 1967). The first novel in Clarke's "Toronto trilogy," The Meeting Point explores Toronto's early struggles with multiculturalism through the experiences of a group of West Indian immigrants.

3. **The Torontonians** by Phyllis Brett Young (Longmans, 1960; reissued by McGill-Queen's University Press, 2007). An international bestseller when first published in 1960, The Torontonians was Canada's first sub-urban satire. Targeting the emptiness of lives consumed with Cuisinarts, wall-to-wall carpets and backyard cookouts, it offered early warning of the consequences of unchecked sprawl.

4. **Strange Fugitive** by Morley Callaghan (Scribners, 1928). Considered the prototypical gangster novel and Canada's first urban novel, Strange Fugitive depicts Toronto as a morally divided city in the jazz era of speakeasies, bootleggers and gangland murder.

5. **The Gerrard Street Mystery** by John Charles Dent (Rose, 1888). This collection of strange tales uncovers the unsettling mysteries swept beneath drawing-room carpets in Victorian Toronto.

CULTURAL INSTITUTIONS

Toronto's first venture into the world of show and tell was possibly Moss Park, the stately and now long-gone Greek Revival home of prominent 19th-century businessman William Allen. Its sumptuous

Nino Ricci

Nino Ricci exemplifies the growing number of Toronto writers who draw on an ethnic background as a literary source of inspiration and exploration. Born to Italian parents, Ricci, in his first novel, 1990's *Lives of the Saints*, provided razor-sharp insights into the Canadian experience of a first-generation Italian-immigrant family.

Lives of the Saints became an instant hit, staying 75 weeks on the national bestseller list, winning the 1990 Governor General's Literary Award for fiction (Ricci won a second time in 2008 for his novel *The Origin of the Species*). *Lives of the Saints* was the first of a trilogy—next were 1993's In a *Glass House* and 1997's *Where She Has Gone*—that followed the narrator, Vittorio Innocentes, for more than 30 years from Italy to southern Ontario, Nigeria and Toronto. At the beginning of the novel, Innocentes voices Ricci's multicultural take on Toronto.

The trilogy became popular enough that in 2004 an Italian-Canadian co-production team adapted it for television as a miniseries. *Lives of the Saints* was broadcast in both countries to acclaim, undoubtedly helped along by the A-list cast, which included Sophia Loren, Kris Kristofferson and Italian-Torontonian Nick Mancuso. Ricci's 2003 novel, *Testament*, a fictional revisionist account of the life of Jesus Christ, posed the formidable risk of paling in comparison to the Bible. His epic tale was so well executed it won Ontario's prestigious Trillium Book Award.

Ricci is an outstanding voice of the new Toronto literati, reflecting the brashness and brawny ambitions of immigrants in the country's most multicultural city. He brings to life a vibrant city far removed from the dour provincialism of Robertson Davies' Toronto and surroundings or the reserved elite of Timothy Findley's Rosedale. Ricci makes his world real to insiders and observers, painting a Toronto that can belong to everyone.

dining room, decorated with stuffed birds in glass cases, was the talk of the town in its day.

Today you can visit more than 120 museums, public archives and public cultural attractions in the Toronto area. They range from the imposingly traditional and long established (the ROM and the AGO) and the ethnic focused (Taras H. Shevechenko Museum, Silverman Heritage Museum) through to the artistic (the Gardiner Museum of Ceramics) to the quirky (the Bata Shoe Museum), the sweetly specialized (Redpath Sugar Museum) and the simply sweet (Riverdale Farm).

- **Art Gallery of Ontario (AGO):** One of the largest art museums in North America, the AGO has been collecting and displaying local and international works of art since 1900. Today it has upward of

TAKE 5 FIVE FESTIVALS
THAT SHOWCASE THE ARTS

1. **North by Northeast (five days in June):** An annual live-music and film festival well into its second decade that features new and established acts. Performances take place in selected Toronto clubs for fans, agents, talent scouts, talent bookers, media reps and record-company executives.

2. **Dream in High Park (late June to early September):** Held every summer under the stars in High Park, this drama festival was launched almost 30 years ago and has attracted 1.3 million theatregoers.

3. **Nuit Blanche (early October):** Toronto imported the dusk-to-dawn arts festival, already popular in Europe, in 2006. Visitors can wander all night for free among a choice of art galleries, museums, schools and artist-run venues to view art and take in performances.

4. **Word On the Street (late September):** This major literary festival, now held in Queen's Park, celebrated its 20th year in 2009. It features readings, booksellers, literacy organizations, libraries, writers' associations and literary magazines.

5. **Luminato (mid-June):** Launched in 2007, the multidisciplinary Luminato brings music, theatre, dance, film, literature, visual arts and design to Toronto stages, streets and public spaces.

68,000 pieces of art in its collection, dating from 100 AD to the present. The building recently underwent a $276-million facelift and redesign by expatriate architect Frank Gehry. The reopening in November of 2008 attracted enormous crowds, and the spectacular new galleries, works of art in themselves, have boosted the art-viewing space by 47 percent.

- **Royal Ontario Museum (ROM):** The ROM is among the world's leading museums of natural history and world cultures. It has some six million objects in its own collection and is a major touring venue for exhibits from around the world. First opened in 1914, the museum expanded with much fanfare into the Daniel Libeskind-designed "Michael Lee-Chin Crystal" in 2007, a multi-storey, intricately designed, interlocking glass-and-steel form that seems to leap out of the older, more stately ROM structure. The Crystal houses eight new galleries, including the largest hall in Canada for international exhibitions.

- **Ontario Science Centre:** The Science Centre celebrated its 40th birthday in 2009, but although it's officially middle-aged now, it's definitely still geared to kids. Science-based exhibits, speakers and movies, plus Ontario's first IMAX Dome theatre, draw more than 40 million visitors every year.

- **Toronto Zoo:** "Canada's premier zoo," according to its literature, sprawls over 287 hectares in Scarborough's Rouge Valley. With 10 km of walking trails and more than 5,000 animals and 460-plus species, it's among the largest in the world. The mega-zoo traces its origins to 1888, when a Toronto alderman donated one live deer to the city for display. Its original venue later became Riverdale Park, where there's now a model farm.

Did you know. . .

that *Night Heat*, *Due South*, *Flashpoint* and all of the *Degrassi* series were filmed in Toronto?

Snow Days

Michael Snow proves the same point first demonstrated by the Group of Seven: it is possible to build a successful artistic career without leaving for New York, Paris or Berlin. Raised in the tony Toronto neighbourhood of Rosedale, Snow attended Toronto's Upper Canada College and was primed to enter Toronto's establishment when he decided, against his parents' wishes, to pursue his childhood talent for art instead. He enrolled in the Ontario College of Art, graduating in 1952 with a design specialization.

After an 18-month stint travelling Europe, Snow set up a studio in Toronto while holding a day job as a film animator. A 1956 solo exhibition of figurative drawings and paintings at Avrom Isaacs's Greenwich Gallery in Toronto launched his artistic career.

Although he lived in Toronto most of his life, Snow did spend time in New York, where he completed his renowned *Walking Women* series of works, which culminated in an 11-part sculpture at Expo 67 in the Ontario Pavilion. In New York Snow established himself as one of the world's foremost avant-garde filmmakers with his 1967 experimental stream-of-consciousness film *Wavelength*. However, New York began to spook Snow and his wife, the artist Joyce Wieland, after she suffered a terrifying mugging. They returned to a safer, and what they called saner, Toronto.

Torontonians best know Snow for public commissions, including *Flight Stop* (1979), a landmark fibreglass sculpture of flying Canadian geese suspended from the glass ceiling of the Eaton Centre. Equally prominent is *The Audience* (1989) at the SkyDome (now the Rogers Centre), a frieze of 14 gold-painted sculptures of larger-than-life-sized cheering sports fans, extending out of the stadium's northeast and northwest corners like revelling gargoyles. Marking Snow's contribution to Toronto culture was his 1994 blockbuster-scale 40-year retrospective, *The Michael Snow Project*, held simultaneously at the Art Gallery of Ontario and the Power Plant gallery.

Snow is clearly one of Canada's major artists. He continues to work as a painter, photographer, filmmaker, sculptor and musician, remaining interested in redefining relationships between media. He has twice been awarded the Order of Canada, first, as an Officer in 1982, then as the even more prestigious Companion in 2007.

THE MAGNIFICENT SEVEN

The Group of Seven was the first collection of artists in the country to explore the nation's identity as something that wasn't largely British influenced or derivative. Most of the members—A. Y. Jackson, Frank Johnston, Arthur Lismer, J. E. H. MacDonald, Frederick Varley, Franklin Carmichael and Lawren Harris—met while working for the Toronto design firm Grip Ltd.

In a country desperately searching for shared experience and meaning in the first few decades of the 1900s, the Group of Seven provided Canadians with art that was unabashedly its own. The landscape artists rendered images that were imbued with feeling, while their painting style rejected the prevailing naturalism for post-impressionism. Through their own and collective efforts, the members helped Canadians appreciate their own art and artists.

Although the group was only together from 1920 to 1933, it had a profound influence on art in Canada; many of the members also taught across the country. Although some of the artistic establishment resented their individual and collective success, the group inspired a whole generation of future artists, showing them that meaning could be found in a "new" country and that they could realistically aspire to making a living from their artistic expression of it.

THE WALK OF FAME

As in Hollywood, Canada's Walk of Fame is a series of star-studded paving blocks, only this stretch of a King Street sidewalk salutes the best in Canadian culture and sports. The likes of Bryan Adams, k.d. lang, Steve Nash, James Cameron, Alex Trebek, Bobby Orr, Anne Murray, Gordon Lightfoot and Gordie Howe are all there—more than 110 red stars (actually stylized maple leafs) in all.

LITERATURE

You could argue that the year Toronto became a writer's town was 1793, as demonstrated by Elizabeth Simcoe's diary entries. A century of lively journalism and poetry followed, and novels set in the city began to appear by the end of the 1800s. Morley Callaghan's 1928 *Strange Fugitive*, set in Toronto, is usually hailed as Canada's first urban novel, but it has several largely forgotten (some would say forgettable) earlier precedents in the city. That early 20th-century flow built to an explosion in content and quality of literary writing and publishing.

Many Toronto writers are international stars and have won a significant number of Governor General Literary Awards since the program was launched in 1937, including:

- Margaret Atwood: 1966, poetry or drama, *The Circle Game*; 1985, fiction, *The Handmaid's Tale*
- Timothy Findley: 1977, fiction, *The Wars*; 2000, drama, *Elizabeth Rex*
- Michael Ondaatje: 1970, prose and poetry, *The Collected Works of Billy the Kid*; 1979, poetry or drama, *There's a Trick With a Knife I'm Learning to Do*; 1992, fiction, *The English Patient*; 2000, fiction, *Anil's Ghost*; 2007, fiction, *Divisadero*
- Nino Ricci: 1990, fiction, *Lives of the Saints*; 2008, fiction, *The Origin of Species*

Source: Canada Council

TORONTO WINNERS OF THE SCOTIABANK GILLER PRIZE

Vincent Lam, for *Bloodletting and Miraculous Cures*	2006
M.G. Vassanji, for *The In-Between World of Vikram Lall*	2003
Austin Clarke, for *The Polished Hoe*	2002
Michael Ondaatje, for *Anil's Ghost*	2000
and David Adams Richards, for *Mercy Among the Children*	
Margaret Atwood, for *Alias Grace*	1996
M.G. Vassanji, for *The Book of Secrets*	1994

Source: ScotiaBank Giller Prize

ALL YOU NEED IS LOVE

One of the world's most prolific publishing houses is romance publisher Harlequin Enterprises, which is based in Toronto. Having shipped a staggering 5.63 billion books since its founding in the late 1940s, Harlequin is and one of the most successful publishing enterprises in the world. It cranks out about 120 titles a month in 29 different languages and is owned by mega-media giant TorStar, parent company of another huge entity in the *Toronto Star*.

FILM INDUSTRY

The disruption caused by film trucks, mobile trailers, cameras and lighting equipment on the streets has grown so commonplace in the last two decades that most Torontonians don't even notice it anymore. Production companies spend more than $800 million filming on location in the city every year. It's also the home of the Canadian Film Centre (CFC), founded in 1988 by award-winning Toronto-born director Norman Jewison.

Did you know. . .

that there's a "Joe Shuster Way" in Toronto, named for the Canadian co-creator of *Superman*? A mint copy of the first *Superman* comic book published in 1938 recently sold at auction for $317,200.

Rush

Despite their superstar status, Rush has often been dismissed by rock critics, which is odd for a band with such a unique sound and singer as well as complex songs and ambitious lyrics. Cookie-cutter they're not, and flash-in-the-pan they surely ain't. Thirty-five years after their first album and major tour, Rush is still going strong.

On the other hand, the members are an unlikely band to have sold over 40 million albums worldwide: they don't record pop ditties or love songs and have a rather unphotogenic front man. Moreover, they're hard to pin down; the progressive-rock, heavy-metal and hard-rock labels all apply. Rush's trademark is their tremendously dense and big sound, which the trio, amazingly, is able to replicate live.

Alex Lifeson is considered a guitar virtuoso, and drummer Neil Peart unites the power bashing of Keith Moon with the complexity of jazz. What truly defines Rush's sound, however, is the high-pitched screech of bassist and keyboardist Geddy Lee. Some people reckon Lee unlistenable; Rush fans disagree about the voice behind rock radio staples "Tom Sawyer" and "Spirit of the Radio."

Rush formed in Toronto in the late 1960s but coalesced in its current form in 1974 when Peart joined the group and the band recorded its first album. Lee and Lifeson had grown up in Toronto, Peart in St. Catherines. The band remains Toronto based; Lifeson and Lee live locally, while Peart now resides in southern California.

Peart is also the author of three books and writes the band's lyrics. In its early days, Rush was known for sci-fi influenced songs, often drawing on literature and mythology. One of Peart's books, 2002's *Ghost Rider: Travels on the Healing Road*, was about his 55,000-mile motorcycle trip across North America in the wake of the death of his teenaged daughter in a car accident, and then his wife's death from cancer.

Rush's *Snakes & Arrows* album came out in 2007, and the band toured extensively behind it; a new disc is in the works. Rush is also finally gaining some respect with rock critics, who concede the band's intelligence, longevity and professionalism, if nothing else.

The Centre provides training, creative partnerships and promotion for budding Canadian directors, writers, producers and editors.

Filmmakers like Toronto because of its variety of locations, low crime rate, talented actors and technicians and film-friendly local government. The city is close to the U.S. border for Americans, and both domestic and foreign production companies that shoot in Toronto can qualify for federal and provincial tax credits.

TAKE 5 JOHN KARASTAMATIS'S FIVE
MUST-SEE TORONTO THEATRES AND EVENTS

John Karastamatis began going to the theatre in Toronto as a teenager when he discovered pay-what-you-can performances. He has promoted and produced theatre for three decades and is currently the director of communications for Mirvish Productions.

1. **The Royal Alexandra Theatre.** The oldest continuously operating legitimate theatre in North America, the Alex has been Toronto's preeminent large-scale theatre since it was built in 1907. Every major international blockbuster show has played here in its Canadian premiere, from *Oklahoma* and *Hair* to *Les Miserables* and *Rent*. And almost every major star has tread the Alex's boards, including Al Jolson, Katherine Hepburn and Donald Sutherland.

2. **The heritage alternative theatres.** In the late 1960s and early '70s, a new generation of nationalists founded companies committed to Canadian theatre—that is, producing theatre written by, created by and performed by Canadians. Three companies—Tarragon Theatre, Factory Theatre and Theatre Passe Murraille—still flourish and all continue to produce great shows and adhere to their original mandates. For a taste of the daring early halcyon days and a real bargain, try a pay-what-you-can performance, offered at Sunday matinees.

3. **The fringe festivals.** These sprouted two decades ago as venues for new artists to do their own stuff; they're new alternatives to the "alternative" theatres, which had become closed-door institutions.

LOCATION FILMING PERMITS

Number issued by year . . .

- 2008: 3,324
- 2007: 3,437
- 2006: 3,659
- 2005: 4,154

Source: Toronto Film & Television Office

Now each summer the Toronto Fringe and Summerworks provide hundreds of independent shows in almost every small and medium-size performance space in the city, presenting a cornucopia of everything you can possibly imagine on stage and then some. The Tony Award-winning musical *The Drowsy Chaperone* was first staged at the Toronto Fringe. More than 50,000 theatregoers clamour for the roughly $10 tickets.

4. **Soulpepper.** A relatively new player, founded in 1998, Soulpepper has quickly become an indispensable part of the theatre scene. Staging classics of the international repertoire of Shakespeare, Chekhov and Ibsen and a few now-classic contemporary plays, Soulpepper has several superb venues in the Distillery District and operates year-round with a company of artists that rank among the best anywhere.

5. **Commercial theatre.** Toronto is the third-largest theatre centre in the English-speaking world, after London and New York, mainly because of its abundant commercial productions. In reality not all of it does make money, but this sector mounts shows in magnificent contemporary and heritage playhouses and employs thousands of artists, artisans, technicians and administrators (including the writer of this list). The main venues are the Alex, the Princess of Wales Theatre, the Elgin and Winter Garden complex, the Sony Centre, the Canon, the Panasonic and the Toronto Centre for the Arts.

FILMING ON LOCATION IN TORONTO

- Major productions: 81.4 percent ($499.2 million)
- Commercials: 12.3 percent ($75.5 million)
- Animation: 5.2 percent ($35.8 million)
- Music videos: 0.5 percent ($3.0 million)

MAJOR PRODUCTIONS IN TORONTO (2008)

- TV series: 66 percent
- Features: 16 percent
- TV specials: 13 percent
- Movies of the week: 5 percent

TORONTO INTERNATIONAL FILM FESTIVAL

The Toronto International Film Festival (TIFF) has become one of the highlights of the social season. Peasants, of course, are entitled—indeed, even encouraged—to attend the shows, but status is conferred on those who will be gracing the most in-demand after parties.

Since the turn of the last century, no art medium has created as many international stars as celluloid, and for 10 glorious days beginning Labour Day weekend, TIFF is the centre of the celluloid universe. For Torontonians, the chance to see the famous and soon-to-be famous is just as important as the films they watch; it's an escape, a time to embrace both art and artifice with both arms.

Master of Gore

On April 1, 2009, filmmaker David Cronenberg received France's most prestigious award, the Légion d'honneur, becoming the first English-Canadian ever to be awarded the prize.

It has been an unlikely journey for Cronenberg, who began dabbling with short avant-garde films while studying English literature at the University of Toronto. After graduating, he had an unusual experience for a Canadian filmmaker: commercial success with lukewarm critical reception. First there was *Shivers* (1975), now a cult classic, followed by *Rabid* (1977), *The Brood* (1979) and *Scanners* (1981)—films establishing him as a director with a darker-than-usual take on horror, a genre that, even in its milder forms, is not typically associated with Canadian cinema.

Cronenberg's first film to garner critical praise, especially in Europe, was 1983's *Videodrome*, which introduced his ongoing concern with the complex relationship between mind and body, and with ethical issues in science and technology. *The Dead Zone*, a film adaptation of Stephen King's novel, was released later that same year. Three years later Cronenberg released *The Fly*, his ambitious remake of the 1958 sci-fi classic film.

Toronto was an important backdrop in Cronenberg's controversial 1996 erotic thriller, *Crash*, based on J.G. Ballard's novel, which won a Cannes Film Festival Special Jury Prize for "originality, daring and audacity." In the film Cronenberg depicts Toronto as a futuristic metropolis of steel, concrete and abandoned freeways.

The director wants his latest production to be Toronto-based too: the $150-million spy thriller for MGM based on Robert Ludlum's 1979 book, *The Matarese Circle*, features Tom Cruise and Denzel Washington. One of the city's best-known filmmakers, Cronenberg has no plans to leave Toronto despite his A-list status.

In 2008, some 312 films—249 features and 63 shorts chosen from more than 3,000 submissions—from 64 countries were screened at downtown cinemas. Slumdog Millionaire's world premiere and People's Choice Award winner at TIFF continued the festival's enviable track record of anticipating Oscar nods.

TAKE 5 — PARMINDER SINGH'S TOP FIVE PUNJABI HOCKEY TERMS

Parminder Singh loves everything about Toronto. He is a co-host of OMNI TV's Chardi Kalaa and host of the Punjabi health show, "Thuadi Sehat." Singh started his broadcasting career as an intern with 680 Sports and is currently the voice of CBC's Hockey Night in Canada: Punjabi Edition. Singh has also called games for NBA's Toronto Raptors and MLS's Toronto FC. He is very passionate about sports and loves being a Torontonian. Sat Sri Akaal (Hello/Goodbye).

1. **Rubber tiki:** Hockey puck. A puck in French is called "rondell." In Punjabi, no such term exists. However, we do have a tasty potato appetizer that is discus in shape, very similar to a puck called an "aloo tiki" (potato tiki). Hence, I decided to use the term "rubber tiki" or just "tiki," very similar in sound to rubber "ducky."

2. **Chapaid shot:** Slap shot! Can also be used in its singular form as, "ooh, he just got a *chapaid* from his momma!"

3. **Chukde phate:** This call is used very loosely as in after a great play. Feel free to say *chukde phate* to a friend, co-worker or employee after a job well done.

4. **Barfing:** Icing. Ice in the Punjabi language translates to "burf." However, there is no plural form for "burf." When icing is the call during the game I use the term "barfing." Here is what a call may sound like when translated into English. "The Leafs *barfed* the puck!"

5. **Mahriaa shot, keeta goal:** You guessed it! I did not forget about Foster Hewitt's iconic phrase "he shoots, he scores!"

They said it

"This is probably the only time in his career that Oscar Peterson has been called a square."
– Dennis Lee, then Toronto's poet laureate, at the June 22, 2004, ceremony announcing the renaming of the Toronto-Dominion Courtyard

Weblinks

Festivals and Events

wx.toronto.ca/festevents.nsf
The city's official festivals-and-events calendar.

Toronto Culture

www.livewithculture.ca
Billing itself as "the ultimate guide to Toronto's culture scene," it lists upcoming events by category and area and provides details on the city's permanent cultural attractions and cultural history.

TAKE5 FIVE FEATURE FILMS
SHOT IN TORONTO

Movies are listed starting with the highest grossing at the box office.
1. *Chicago* (2002), with Catherine Zeta-Jones, Renee Zellweger and Richard Gere
2. *Three Men and a Baby* (1987), with Tom Selleck, Steve Guttenberg and Ted Danson
3. *X-men* (2000), with Hugh Jackman and Halle Berry
4. *The Santa Clause* (1994), with Tim Allen
5. *Good Will Hunting* (1997), with Robin Williams, Matt Damon and Ben Affleck

Source: Toronto Film and Television Office

Food

There may not be an indigenous Toronto cuisine, but make no mistake, this is a food-lover's city. As you might expect from the most multicultural city in the world, more than 8,000 restaurants abound, offering a mind-boggling array of culinary choices.

Ethnic diversity and food are what define the Toronto food experience, and not just in predictable ways. Toronto restaurants are constantly evolving, in tandem with a defined foodie culture and influences, both local and international, that take tea, brunch, dinner and local sustainability seriously.

Some of Toronto's best international-cuisine dining destinations include the Danforth, North America's largest Greek neighbourhood, which has arguably the best-known "restaurant strip" in the city. The Danforth is at its best in the summer, when the patios are crowded until the wee hours of the morning and festivals such as the Krinos Taste of the Danforth transform the streets with a Mediterranean flair.

For authentic Chinese food, head for Spadina Avenue, from College to Queen, where rows of dim sum restaurants feature waitresses pushing carts with a range of authentic delicacies. For Asian food with a bit more spice, go east to Little India around Greenwood and Coxwell.

Yorkville is the best bet for fine dining with celebrities and the pretty people. Its cluster of high-end restaurants (names and venues change as frequently as the latest fashion trends) attracts movie stars and the well-heeled, especially during the Toronto International Film Festival in September.

At the other end of the spectrum are the city's many diners and

Kensington Market

The story of Kensington Market is a colourful and vibrant one that captures many aspects of early immigration to Toronto. A large estate known as the Ward occupied the area west of Spadina Avenue and around Baldwin Street until 1850, when it was subdivided and row houses were built for Irish and Scottish labourers. Many of these homes still stand and have been occupied by successive waves of immigrants.

By the 1920s, the Ward was too overcrowded to hold the numbers of Jewish immigrants arriving from Eastern Europe and Russia. They began to move west, and by the end of the 1930s about 60,000 lived in the area bounded by Spadina, Dundas, Bathurst and College. Most were Orthodox Jews who had been driven from their rural villages by persecution. Thirty synagogues sprung up in the area to serve the community.

It was common for homeowners to live upstairs in the closely packed two- and three-storey structures and open a shop on the ground floor. Bakers, barbers, furriers, tailors, shoemakers, bankers and pawnbrokers opened businesses, and a flourishing outdoor market sold a diversity of produce, much of which was imported from various homelands. The area soon became known as the Jewish Market.

In the 1950s, the Jewish population moved north and Portuguese immigrants moved in. The newcomers painted their brick houses bright colours and decorated their front yards with religious icons. Kensington Market backyards bloomed with greasy spoons. The most famous are Fran's (its flagship, which dates back to the 1940s, is at College and Yonge) and Shopsy's deli and restaurant, a downtown mainstay. Other Toronto classics include Barberians on Elm (a traditional steakhouse), The Real Jerk on Queen East (spicy Jamaican cuisine) and Dangerous Dan's burgers (which offers the "Coronary Burger," allegedly the biggest hamburger in the city).

grapevines, vegetables and flowers. It took on the feel of a Portuguese town, with rice, beans, vegetables, fruit and nuts being sold outdoors. Meat, fish and cheese stores mingled with travel agencies, repair shops, beauty salons and dozens of other small enterprises. The Portuguese bookstore became a hangout for men who wanted to listen on the radio to soccer games being played in Portugal.

By the 1970s, the Portuguese community was moving west to Little Portugal. Though their meat, fish and cheese shops remained, the proximity of Chinatown and the arrival of new waves of immigrants from the Caribbean, Vietnam and Africa created a more ethnically diverse Market.

In recent years, there have been some signs that the character of the Market as a working-class immigrant neighbourhood is declining. The old-style ethnic businesses now share Kensington Market with upscale cafes, head shops, a small supermarket and an energetic arts community. But despite its growing reputation as a tourist attraction, it remains a practical place for both locals and university students to shop on the cheap.

A CBC-TV show called *King of Kensington* aired from 1975 to 1980; legendary Canadian actor Al Waxman starred in the tile role. After Waxman's death in 2001 at age 65, a statue of him was erected in Bellevue Square. In 2006 Kensington Market was designated a National Historic Site.

TORONTO FOOD GLOSSARY

Armageddon Wings is the apt name for the highest spice level (that would be 850,000 Scoville heat units) of the chicken wings served by Duff's Famous Wings. Duff's offers eight levels of spiciness but reserves ringing its in-house alarm for the Armageddon Wings orders.

Butter tarts, which originated in Ontario in the early 1900s, are served in bakeries all over Toronto. The small pastry shell is filled with a mixture of butter, sugar and egg and may include raisins and be topped by a pecan, all baked until golden brown. Try Dufflet Bakery (2638 Yonge St. or 787 Queen St. West) or Queen of Tarts (283 Roncesvalles Ave.) for some of the city's best.

Coffee porter is an intense coffee-flavoured porter produced by Mill Street Brewery in the Distillery District. Its brew has cult status in Toronto and is made with coffee beans from local coffee shop Balzac's.

The Coronary Burger is one of Toronto's best-known novelty-food disasters served at Dangerous Dan's: a burger with two 8-oz burger patties, four slices of bacon, two slices of cheddar and a fried egg on top, with a side of fries and gravy. The diner's Collosal Colon Clogger Combo is a 24-oz burger with a quarter-pound of cheese, bacon and two fried eggs. A steady diet of the same is not recommended.

Dufflet Pastries is a Toronto purveyor of baked goods and the go-to place for birthday cakes. Its plentiful offerings that go far beyond simple butter-cream flavourings, along with sweets such as chocolate-drizzled butter tarts, make Dufflet's a favourite.

Did you know...

that the ground-floor bathroom of Bright Pearl Restaurant on Spadina Ave. in Chinatown is believed to be haunted?

TAKE 5 FIVE BEST
ARTISAN CHEESE SHOPS

1. **Global Cheese**, 76 Kensington Ave.
2. **Cheese Magic**, 182 Baldwin Ave.
3. **Cheese Emporium**, 245 Mount Pleasant Rd.
4. **Cheese Boutique**, 45 Ripley Ave.
5. **Thin Blue Line**, 93 Roncesvalles Ave.

The Gucci Burger is the street-side nickname for the Bymark Burger on the menu at the upscale Bymark restaurant in Toronto's financial district (66 Wellington St. West). The burger is made with 8-oz USDA prime beef with *brie de meaux*, grilled king mushrooms, shaved truffles and onion rings on the side.

Jamie Kennedy's french fries are famous in Toronto and beyond (much to the chagrin of a certain *Hell's Kitchen's* and *Kitchen Nightmares* host). Visit Chef Jamie Kennedy's Gilead Café (4 Gilead Place) or Jamie Kennedy Wine Bar (9 Church St.) for a taste of his famous frites, naked or dressed as poutine.

Kimchi Empanadas. Where else in the world would you be able to find a fusion of spicy pickled Korean cabbage with a Mexican flair? At El Gordo Fine Foods in Kensington Market, you can get empanadas in 42 flavours, including kimchi.

North America's best BBQ pork may or may not be found in Toronto, but the phrase is widely known and associated with Kom Jug Yuen Restaurant (371 Spadina), one of Toronto's hole-in-the-wall Chinese restaurants that serves mediocre barbeque pork but is cheap, fast and great for students.

O&B stands for the Oliver-and-Bonacini brand, a top name in the Toronto restaurant industry. O&B restaurants include upscale Canoe, often touted as the city's best restaurant; Auberge du Pommier, with a French flair; fun food at Jump; casual fare at Biff's Bistro; and modern-classy dining at Oliver & Bonacini Café Grill.

TAKE 5 LINDA LEATHERDALE'S FIVE PLACES TO POWER LUNCH

Linda Leatherdale moved to Toronto from Orillia at age 18 with a dream to make it big—and she did. A TV host, author, popular financial commentator and seminar expert, she was the feisty and outspoken financial editor for *The Toronto Sun* for several years and remains a no-nonsense advocate for working folk. She has led tax crusades, fought for consumers' rights, influenced politicians, had laws passed and made both friends and foes in high places.

1. **Biagio Italian Restaurant:** Former prime ministers dine here, as do top CEOs and Eddie Greenspan, the eminent lawyer whose office is right across the street (he always gets the best seat, in the window). There are many reasons the rich and famous—John Turner, Rex Murphy, Paul Godfrey and Allan Fotheringham, among them—are loyal to Biagio. Owner Biagio Vinci, who hails from Italy, offers an exquisite menu of authenic Italian fare. And there's the historic setting and, in summer, a romantic courtyard with a candlelit fountain. But for most, it's the man himself; every year on the Sunday before Christmas, Biagio opens his fine restaurant to feed the homeless.

2. **Canoe Restaurant and Bar:** From Bay Street brokers and CEOs to the international business elite, this restaurant high atop the TD Bank Tower is a favourite for corporate movers and shakers. It's ranked as one of Canada's best, and the five-star menu features Canadian fish, game and produce as well as Canadian wines. What's more, you get a great view of Toronto.

Peameal-bacon sandwiches, a Toronto institution, are proudly made with Canadian peameal back bacon. You can find the best versions at the St. Lawrence Market.

3. **North 44:** The first time I dined at this upscale Yonge Street restaurant named after Toronto's latitude was with *Sun* staffers giving former board member Ron Osborne a fond farewell. We ate, drank and were merry, enjoying the exquisite gourmet dining (try the lobster risotto), five-star service and atmosphere and unbelievable wine list. We even used publisher Paul Godfrey's credit card to send a bottle of champagne to the table of former Maple Leafs' coach Pat Burns, who was celebrating his wife's birthday (oops, I don't think we told Godfrey...)

4. **Centro Restaurant and Lounge:** I first visited Centro in the 1980s when a restaurateur friend was in town doing research and wanted to find out firsthand how Centro was revolutionizing the industry. Well into the millennium, it remains a dining hot spot for Toronto's who's who. It boasts a liberating five-star North American menu and service, and the wine list is out of this world.

5. **Flow Restaurant and Lounge:** Tony Longo, the man behind Centro, has now opened Flow with a partner, a classy dining establishment and magical Yorkville gem. With its vibrant LED-projected exterior, a two-level interior and a large glass-enclosed waterfall, plus a stunning 60-seat patio, Flow is the perfect place to catch a glimpse of the who's who and such celebrities as actor Dan Aykroyd. The menu is continental, with a progressive North America style.

Pho, often called "Fo" but properly pronounced "Fe," is the name of authentic Vietnamese restaurants and a Vietnamese noodle-soup dish found all over Toronto. Try Golden Turtle/Pho Rua Vang (125 Ossington Ave.) for some of the best Pho in the GTA.

Steam Whistle Pilsner, another favourite local brew, has been in production since March of 2000 and is known as Canada's premium pilsner. The brewery is located a stone's throw from the Air Canada Centre, the Rogers Centre and the CN Tower in a historic Canadian Pacific Rail steam-locomotive repair shop.

Street eats from around the world. Toronto's bylaws are stringent when it comes to street-side food, but there's no lack of "street meat," or hot dog stands/carts/trucks, around the city. In May of 2009, a number of street vendors offering Korean, Greek, Caribbean and Thai options will launch operations on Toronto streets.

TAKE 5 BLOGTO.COM'S FIVE BEST PIZZA SLICES IN TORONTO

1. **Bitondo Pizzeria & Sandwiches** (11 Clinton St.): Probably the only pizza place in the world that doesn't deliver, but the pepperoni slices prove they don't need to.
2. **Cora Pizza** (649 Spadina Ave.): A favourite of University of Toronto students looking for a late-night slice.
3. **Amato Pizza** (429A Yonge St. and other locations): One of Toronto's first unconventional pizza shops with chicken, broccoli, spinach and garlic options.
4. **Pizzaiolo** (270 Adelaide St. West and other locations): Personal pan-size pizzas with some of the best crust in Toronto, filled with a variety of toppings and golden-crusted edges.
5. **Papa Ceo** (645 Spadina Ave.): Known for big soft slices of pizza overflowing with toppings.
Source: BlogTO.com

Sushi pizza is a recent craze. The "pizza crust" is made of rice that has been shaped into a disc and fried lightly on each side. Toppings include any combination of sushi choices, including salmon, tuna, avocado and tobiko.

TAKE 5 JAMIE KENNEDY'S FIVE WAYS
TORONTO INSPIRES HIS MENU

One of Canada's most celebrated chefs, Jamie Kennedy graduated from George Brown College's cook apprenticeship program in 1977; he now owns and operates Jamie Kennedy Kitchens and has launched several of Toronto's landmark restaurants, including Scaramouche and the Palmerston Restaurant. Kennedy is known for his commitment to environmental issues and his support for organic agriculture, local producers and traditional methods.

1. I find inspiration in the markets of our city's neighbourhoods. From Gerrard East to St. Clair West, from Kensington to Steeles and pockets in between, you can circumnavigate the planet on the TTC.

2. I like the potential for finding exotic street food here. A popular item on my menu is called "streets of Toronto" — it's three tastings of "street food" from around the world.

3. The people I hire in my establishments come from all over, and the longer they stay with me, the more the likelihood of something unusual showing up on my menu, like hoppers and curry, an invention of Tamil culture.

4. It gives me the opportunity to engage in a local food culture whose aim is to render a cuisine that, because of its ethnic diversity, will be unique to this place.

5. I am tradition-less, or like a sponge for tradition, because in my family there really was no tradition in cooking to adhere to. This allows me to explore, combine, synthesize and create something unique with impunity or, at least, no bias.

TAKE 5 GIZELLE LAU'S TOP FIVE
SPOTS FOR A TORONTO COFFEE BREAK

Gizelle Lau, a born-and-raised Torontonian with a passion for travel, food and wine, has made her career in travel writing for and, in particular, about Toronto's food and wine culture. From Montreal and Bangkok to Cuba, she's always searching for a great cup of coffee, planning her next meal or plotting an itinerary for her next world jaunt.

1. **Le Gourmand** (152 Spadina Ave.) has great coffee and fresh baked goods all day long. An Americano is the perfect pairing for its amazing chocolate-chip cookies, which are the size of your head. You can't help but feel right at home in this bustling shop.

2. **Moonbeam Coffee** (30 St. Andrew St., in Kensington Market) is for artists and bohemians looking for top-of-the-line fair trade coffee, rare blends and an extensive selection, without the artificial coffee-shop feel. It has a great patio in the front and back. The cappuccinos and chai lattes are some of the city's best.

3. **Balzac's** (50 Mill St., Building 60 in the Distillery District) has the best coffee-shop atmosphere in all of Toronto because it's set in an old building that was once part of the Gooderham and Worts Distillery in the 1800s. Cozy with character, the café serves great iced coffees to sip on the patio during the summer.

4. **Manic Coffee** (426 College St., in Little Italy) and Dark Horse Espresso Bar (682 Queen St. East) both serve delicious lattes and espressos by award-winning baristas but are winners in their own right by serving direct trade coffee—purchased straight from the grower, even better than fair trade.

5. **Dessert Trends** (154 Harbord St.) is great for a relaxing coffee or tea with beautiful and delicious desserts on the side in a clean, crisp and modern-style cafe-bistro. This one's for someone in dire need of satisfying a sweet tooth alongside a caffeine fix.

TORONTO'S FAST-FOOD CULTURE

McDonald's has approximately 50 restaurants in the Greater Toronto Area and 515 in Ontario. The busiest in Canada is located just west of Toronto in Cambridge, on Canada's busiest highway, the 401.

At the beginning of 2009, there were 1,001 **Starbucks** in the country and about 145 in the GTA, just under half of them in the downtown core.

Tim Hortons has a fiercely loyal customer base: more than 40 percent of customers visit this fast-food coffee/donut/sandwich shop four times or more every week. As of the end of 2008, there were 2,917 Tim Hortons restaurants in Canada, about 1 percent of them in the downtown T.O. core alone, accounting for roughly 42 percent of Canada's fast-food service.

FOOD NEIGHBOURHOODS

Baldwin Village is a microcosm of Toronto's cultural and culinary mix. Italian, French, Korean, Japanese, Chinese, Vietnamese, Mexican, vegetarian and organic restaurants are all available within an easy neighbourhood stroll.

A handful of **Chinatowns** are located across the city, from "old Chinatown" downtown (Spadina and Dundas) to hubs in the north-end suburbs of Scarborough and Markham (check out Pacific Mall at Kennedy and Steeles for a one-of-a-kind experience). Chinese-Torontonians often argue you can find better dim sum in the city than in Hong Kong.

The Danforth (Greektown) has low- to high-end souvlaki, but the Greek coffee is a killer for those addicted to Tim Hortons. Most establishments feature authentic Greek cuisine: broiled lamb, calamari or saganaki (flaming cheese served table-side by a waiter bellowing "Opa!").

Distillery District. Toronto's cobblestone district of art galleries, photography studios and boutiques is also home to Balzac's Coffee (Building No. 60), a specialty chocolate factory and shop (Soma Chocolatemaker, Building No. 47) and the Mill Street Brewery (Building No. 63), all favourite destinations for as different reasons as there are palates.

Kensington Market, with reggae in the streets, green Chilean sausages, fruit-and-vegetable stands, jam-packed cheese shops, great bakeries and coffee, as well as vegetarian, hip and Mexican-influenced restaurants, is a one-of-a-kind destination.

Koreatown is where you'll find some of the best-prepared meat in Toronto, marinated and seasoned to Korean perfection. Each shop has its own pork-bone soup recipe, but Owl of Minerva is famous, as are the walnut-cake shops in this neighbourhood at Bloor Street West and Christie Street.

Little India is the only place where Torontonians of Indian descent will swear by the butter chicken.

Little Italy offers Italian food for all budgets and tastes but is especially good for its patio scene, romantic moments and pizza. Try the hole-in-the-wall institution Bitondo's (11 Clinton St.) for the best pizza, where you can watch Mario Bitondo throw your pizza dough himself.

Did you know. . .

that the best places to catch celebrities and movie stars during the Toronto International Film Festival are at Mark McEwan's ONE restaurant, Rain, Flow, Lobby Bar at the Four Seasons and Ultra Supper Club in Yorkville?

Little Portugal has all the passion and soul of Lisbon, and you can be sure the streets, bars and restaurants will be packed when World Cup Soccer rolls around.

Roncesvalles, or Little Poland, is the place to find homemade Polish food: beet soup with dumplings,schnitzel, polish sausages, cabbage rolls and paczkis (traditional Polish doughnuts).

TAKE 5 WENDY GOLDMAN'S FIVE BEST
BRUNCHES IN THE CITY

Toronto native Wendy Goldman received her master's degree in journalism abroad before returning to write about life and culture in her hometown. The online editor for Torstar Digital's interactive city guide writes regularly about the city's food culture.

1. **Aunties and Uncles** (74 Lippincott St.). This is a hideaway off the busy College Street strip, where the renowned potato salad is heavy on the dill and the atmosphere is low on pretension.

2. **Cantine** (138 Avenue Rd.). Ideal for brunch that's a little more upscale and uptown, Cantine has the unique ability to cater to different crowds who hail from trendy Yorkville and the student-oriented Annex. Many rave about the outstanding eggs Benedict and roasted-pear-and-brie frittata.

3. **Saving Grace** (907 Dundas St. West). Saccharine addicts rejoice at this tiny west-end brunch spot that serves legendary caramelized banana French toast.

4. **Bonjour Brioche** (812 Queen St. East). This East End institution lures brunch enthusiasts with its French-inspired cuisine, creatively crafted quiches and baskets of what it bills as Toronto's best croissants.

5. **Boom Breakfast & Co.** (808 College St. West). Boom is a locally owned breakfast chain that serves delicious waffles and steaming cups of coffee for those waiting in line.

TORONTO'S CELEBRITY FOOD CULTURE

Thanks to the growth of Toronto's cosmopolitan food-and-dining scene, paired with the increasing popularity of Food Network Canada, a true foodie culture has emerged over the the past 10 to 15 years. With the rise of such a culture many chefs, food experts and personalities have earned celebrity status in the city's engaged and eager food community.

Anna Olson could be called Toronto's (and Canada's) sweetest celebrity chef, thanks to *Sugar*, her popular TV series on Food Network Canada. You can find her and her husband, chef Michael Olson, at their new shop, Olson Foods, at Ravine Vineyards in Niagara-on-the-Lake or at most Toronto wine/food festivals and events. Olson's latest TV series, Fresh, promotes using local ingredients with a farm-to-table focus.

Bonnie Stern is a legend in Toronto and beyond for her knowledge about food and the many ways she shares it. The author of cookbooks, food columns and media appearances about all things edible, she's also the founder of the Bonnie Stern School of Cooking, which has been offering classes and bringing in celebrity guests for more than 30 years, and its associated Cookware Shop, a food-retail mecca.

Brad Long, recognized worldwide for his work, is the executive chef at the Air Canada Centre's three restaurants and exclusive Platinum Club. You can watch him share what he knows on the Food Network Canada show *Restaurant Makeover*.

Jamie Kennedy is one of the city's most well-known chefs and has more to boast about than his fries. From Gilead Café to the Gardiner Museum and Jamie Kennedy Wine Bar, he's known as a forerunner in using locally sourced and organic ingredients and in revolutionizing the wine scene.

Joanne Kates has been the food critic for *The Globe and Mail* for more than 20 years. She is well-known and respected in the Toronto food community and is notoriously known to have been able to stay unrecognizable to the public.

Kevin Brauch drinks his way around the world by trying new wines, beers and spirits. Although he worked as a bartender at Mr. Greenjeans while attending school in Toronto, today he frequents Paupers Pub in the Annex when he's not travelling for his TV show, *The Thirsty Traveler*, or acting as the floor reporter on *Iron Chef America* alongside Alton Brown.

Marc Thuet is adored for bringing his French-Alsatian flavours and a passion for charcuterie and cured meats to Toronto. His main restaurant, Bite Me!, offers tapas; the newer Petite Thuet prepares rustic dishes. Atelier Thuet is where city chefs chill out after hours.

Mark McEwan is not only one of Toronto's best chefs but also one of its premier restaurateurs, with Bymark, North 44 (which also offers Toronto's most expensive catering) and ONE restaurant in his pocket already. McEwan's fine-food grocery store was set to open in 2009.

Susur Lee is considered one of Toronto's and Canada's best chefs. Introduced to popular culture through his face-off with Bobby Flay on *Iron Chef America* years ago (they tied), he is known for his ferocity in the kitchen (he's a madman for perfection) and his signature ponytail. Find him at Madeline's or Lee—or in New York City at his newest restaurant, Shang.

Did you know...

that Woody Harrelson dines at Colborne Lane when visiting Toronto?

They said it

"We define ourselves by our eclecticism, our many ethnically diverse neighbourhoods. And this variety is strangely liberating. It allows me to take a foreign visitor to Thuet or to Sushi Kaji (the best Japanese restaurant in North America) or to Lai Wah Heen for avant-garde Cantonese dim sum and still feel I'm giving them a genuine Toronto experience."

– James Chatto, Toronto-based restaurant critic and internationally renowned author of several food-related books, including *The Seducer's Cookbook* and *The Man Who Ate Toronto: Memoirs of a Restaurant Lover*

TORONTO BREWPUBS

Amsterdam Brewing Company (21 Bathurst St.)

Amsterdam Brewery, Toronto's first brewpub, has been making craft ales and lagers since 1986. It's known for attracting both beer enthusiasts and patio-goers to its large space at the foot of Bathurst Street.

Granite Brewery (245 Eglinton Ave. East)

Voted "Toronto's best brewpub—ales" by *Toronto Life* magazine, this midtown establishment uses natural ingredients in its brewing process. Granite is known for its British-style ales, stouts and bitters, as well as its delicious pub-style fare.

Did you know...

that at Ed's Real Scoop ice-cream parlour in the Beach, Ed bakes an apple pie for the sole purpose of mashing it up for his apple-pie ice cream, and that you can sample as many flavours as you like?

Mill Street Brewery (55 Mill St.)

Founded in 2002, Mill Street was the first commercial brewery to open in more than a century in downtown's East End and has 13 handcrafted beers on tap. Mill Street won the Canadian Brewery of the Year Award in both 2007 and 2008. Its brews are now sold across Toronto at the Beer Store and LCBO.

Weblinks

TorontoLife.com

www.torontolife.com

The ultimate guide to food culture, restaurants and eating.

OurFaves.com

www.ourfaves.com

Expert and user reviews on restaurants, local highlights, nightlife, attractions, arts and entertainment and shopping.

BlogTO.com

www.blogto.com

Daily source of what's happening in the city, with lots of restaurant reviews and lists of the Best of Toronto, including dim sum, cookies, pizza and coffee shops.

Economy

The country's economic juggernaut, Toronto accounts for 10 percent of total Canadian GDP. To put this in perspective, it would require the cities of New York, Chicago, Boston and San Francisco combined to account for a similar percentage of the American GDP.

Toronto has more head offices, financial and business companies, law firms and accounting firms than anywhere else in the country. It has the largest concentration of medical/pharmaceutical companies and the most research institutions, is the leading printing-and-publishing centre in English-speaking Canada and has more media outlets than any other city. It also has a major food-and-beverage sector, one of the largest film-and-television industries outside Hollywood and the third-largest IT sector in North America that's the fourth largest in the world.

Toronto's economic ascendancy has been gradual. In 1832, Toronto (then York) replaced Kingston as the most important centre in Upper Canada. As a result it attracted government money, and so began the development of Toronto's port and its network of roads. The arrival of railways in the 1850s made it easier to transport an increasing array of goods. Much of Toronto's growth stems from its location; today it's the geographical bridging ground in Canada, located within a one-day drive of 50 percent of the U.S. population.

The establishment of a stock exchange in 1852 served as another catalyst for Toronto's economic development. Factories began to multiply, and a growing financial sector backed lumber, farming and mining both in Ontario and across the country. Immigration supplied businesses with workers, and by the early 1920s Toronto's population topped half a million, growing to nearly 700,000 by 1941.

Throughout much of the 20th century, there was an unspoken competition between Toronto and Montreal as both centres vied for economic importance and supremacy. By the mid-1960s, Toronto was able to claim more national head offices than Montreal for the first time. With the election of René Lévesque in 1976, the competition was over. Capital and people fled the uncertainty of the Quebec political situation and Toronto surpassed Montreal as the most important economy in the country, becoming at the same time Canada's most populous city.

Toronto today has one of the most modern and dynamic city economies in the world, supported by North America's highest concentration of fibre optics. The combination of industry and a highly educated workforce have made the Toronto Census Metropolitan Area (CMA) the second-fastest major employment region in North America and one of the most successful city economies in the world.

Did you know. . .

that the first "skyscraper" in Canada was Toronto's Simpson's department store at the corner of Yonge and Queen streets? Its six storeys reaching 33 metres high were built on a self-supporting steel skeleton structure, the technical qualification for skyscraper designation. Downright Lilliputian compared to today's towers, it was considered an urban marvel when it was built in 1895.

Did you know...

that the King-Bay Chaplaincy in the TD Bank Tower is well positioned, both by location and because of the experience of its chaplains, to offer spiritual solace to financial-district employees? One chaplain, Bruce Smith, is a former captain of the Toronto Argonauts, a former top realtor and broker and now an ordained minister.

GDP

Gross Domestic Product is the total value of goods and services produced in a given time period. Figures below are for 2007, except where noted.

Canada total GDP (2008 estimate)	$1.336 trillion
Ontario GDP	$586.49 billion
Toronto GDP	$133 billion
Toronto CMA GDP	$267 billion
Toronto GDP per capita	$50,156.50
Per capita GDP in Canada (2008)	$40,200
Canadian GDP growth (2008)	0.7 percent
Toronto's percentage of provincial pop.	21 percent
Toronto's share of federal GDP	10 percent
Rate of Toronto's GDP growth (2007)	2.5 percent (for the CMA)
Rate of Toronto's GDP growth (forecast 2008)	2.5 percent (for the CMA)

Source: City of Toronto

Did you know...

that the Royal Bank Plaza's golden windows are actually gold? They're coated in a thin layer of the precious metal, about 2,500 ounces in all.

TAXES
- Provincial sales tax (Ontario): 8 percent
- GST (federal sales tax): 5 percent

Federal Personal Income Taxes, 2009
- First $38,832 of taxable income: 15 percent
- Next $38,832 of taxable income (on the portion between $38,832 and $77,664): 22 percent
- Next $48,600 of taxable income (on the portion between $77,664 and $126,264): 26 percent
- Taxable income over $126,264: 29 percent

Provincial Personal Income Taxes, 2009:
- First $36,848 of taxable income: 6.05 percent
- Next $36,850 of taxable income: 9.15 percent
- On the amount over $73,698: 11.16 percent

Source: Canada Revenue Agency

TAX FREEDOM DAY
The Fraser Institute determines "tax-freedom day" by adding up all local, provincial and federal taxes, then comparing the totals to average provincial incomes to determine on which date taxpayers' earnings stop going out as taxes and start staying in their pockets.

- Alberta — May 28
- New Brunswick — June 3
- Prince Edward Island — June 4
- Manitoba — June 8
- **Ontario** — **June 9**
- Nova Scotia — June 12
- British Columbia — June 13
- Quebec — June 19
- Saskatchewan — June 20
- Newfoundland and Labrador — June 30

Bay Street

There was a time—in 1797, say—when Bay Street was simply a connector lane in a small settlement, linking much more important streets such as Lot Street (now Queen Street West) to the harbour. Today, of course, there is perhaps no street name as well known to Torontonians—or for that matter, to Canadians—as Bay Street, which is the heart of the country's financial system.

Toronto's financial-services sector is the largest contributor to the local economy, accounting for some 17 percent of the city's gross municipal product. It is the second-largest employer in Toronto, with more than 220,000 people working in the sector directly and driving more than 300,000 jobs in business services that are linked to financial services. One in three city accountants and lawyers specializes in financial-services transactions.

Bay Street is home to Canada's five largest banks, and 90 percent of the foreign banks operating in the country have their headquarters in Toronto. Six of the top 10 Canadian insurers—three of which are among the 10 largest in the world, with responsibility for 90 percent of the industry's total assets—have Toronto head offices.

Eighty-five of the country's mutual fund companies, with $400 billion in assets under management—put in perspective, that's 117 times the gross provincial product of Prince Edward Island—and 85 percent of the world's mutual fund companies are located here. The city also is home to 65 percent of Canadian pension fund managers and half of Canada's venture capital firms. The Toronto Stock Exchange (TSX) that serves as the daily barometer for the country is the third largest in North America and seventh largest in the world. The TSX is also the global leader in listings of mining and oil and gas firms.

Bay Street continues to grow apace. Employment growth in the sector has averaged almost five percent since 2000. Bay Street fortunes are the foundations of many a grand cottage built in the Muskokas, shopping trips to New York City, private schools and European vacations. In many respects, as Bay Street goes, so goes Toronto and the rest of the country.

Bay Street Lingo

Green, scratch, lucre, coin, dough, dinero, greenback, bread, bucks, loot, moola, shekels. However you name your dollar, the pursuit of money is nowhere more crystallized than on Bay Street. For newcomers hoisting a pint, sipping an aperitif or enjoying some of the area's fine dining, we supply you with this Bay Street primer for your eavesdropping pleasure.

Bear trap: What happens when a declining market quickly reverses direction and catches short sellers off guard, eventually forcing them to buy back stock at higher prices to cover their positions.

Bo Derek: A "perfect 10" of a stock or investment.

Boiler room: A derogatory term for a place of business, often a brokerage firm, where high-pressure telemarketing tactics are used in sales.

Castles in the sky: How investors describe the market when stock prices are extremely overvalued and unjustifiable according to anticipated future increases in earnings.

Dead-cat bounce: The slight upward bounce that follows a stock's or the market's substantial drop.

Goldilocks economy: An economy that's not too hot, not too cold, just right.

Greater fool theory: There will always be someone—an even greater fool—who will overpay for a stock that is already overpriced.

Iceberg: A verb that means to sell a stock slowly, as if it were an iceberg melting.

January barometer: A forecasting theory that if the S&P 500 is up in January, the stock market will stay up for the rest of the year.

Jitney: A fraudulent investment practice in which two investors trade shares of a security back and forth to give a false indication of high trading activity.

Misery index: The unemployment rate plus the inflation rate.

Killer bee: Usually an investment banker who helps a company avoid a hostile takeover.

October effect: A theory that says that stocks will decline during the month of October. Those who believe in the October effect note that many, if not all, of the major stock market crashes have happened in October.

Puke: To sell a losing stock, even if the loss is substantial.

Quadruple witching hour: The final hour of trading on a Friday when stock-index futures, single stock futures, stock-index options and stock options all expire at the same time. This happens on the third Friday in March, June, September and December.

Seven sisters: Involved in most of Canada's financial transactions of importance, the seven sisters are seven highly successful law firms with head offices in Toronto.

Siliconaires: Dot-com entrepreneurs in their 20s and 30s who found themselves suddenly rich thanks to stock options from their Silicon Valley Internet companies.

Woody: Describes the market when it has a strong and quick upward movement.

Yard: One billion units of a given currency.

Yo-yo: A very volatile market.

Zombie: A company that is insolvent or facing bankruptcy but continues to operate before a merger or foreclosure. It is "living yet dead," because although it clearly can operate, it is not expected to continue to do so.

HOUSEHOLD INCOME: SELECTED CITIES

City (rank)	Household income	Discretionary income	Unemployment rate
Oakville (2)	$134,373	29.1 percent	4.6 percent
Edmonton (18)	$87,941	20.4 percent	3.8 percent
Toronto (23)	**$81,725**	**24.5 percent**	**7.3 percent**
Vancouver (35)	$75,854	23.7 percent	4.5 percent
Halifax (47)	$70,969	24.7 percent	5.2 percent
Winnipeg (65)	$66,779	25.8 percent	4.7 percent
Corner Brook (104)	$60,741	23.4 percent	11.1 percent
Montreal (135)	$54,689	21.1 percent	9.9 percent

Source: Canadian Business Online, 2008

BY THE HOUR

The average hourly wage of employees (not including the self-employed) in the Toronto CMA in 2008 was $21.70. The average median wage was $19/hour. The breakdown was:

- Age 15 to 24 $12.69
- Age 25 and older $23.68
- Men $23.64
- Women $19.98
- Unionized $24.84
- Non-unionized $20.43

Source: Statistics Canada, City of Toronto

Did you know...

that for decades shoppers would rub the left toe of the bronze statue of Timothy Eaton at Eaton's Queen Street flagship store for good luck? The sculpture was a 50th anniversary gift from Eaton's employees to the family, given in 1919 to honour the Eatons' support and generosity during the First World War. You can still rub T. E.'s toe, but you have to go to the Eaton Court at the Royal Ontario Museum to do it now.

You Said How Much?

Occupational title	Average hourly wage in Toronto
Dentist	$59.01
Optometrist	$41.81
Pharmacist	$40.80
Computer and information services manager	$37.10
Physiotherapist	$34.00
Financial auditor and accountant	$30.96
Lawyer	$30.05
Registered nurse	$29.55
Electrical engineer	$27.95
Secondary school teacher	$27.60
Financial and investment analyst	$26.20
Social worker	$26.05
Architect	$25.45
Sales, marketing and advertising manager	$24.65
Biologist and natural scientist	$23.95
Journalist	$23.10
Insurance adjuster and claims examiner	$22.95
Web designer and developer	$21.65
Plumber	$21.15
Payroll clerk	$19.50
Legal secretary	$18.75
Truck driver	$17.90
Medical secretary	$16.45
Banking, insurance and other financial clerks	$15.85
Foundry worker	$13.40
Receptionist and switchboard operator	$13.15
Data-entry clerk	$12.80
Restaurant and food-service manager	$12.55
Hotel front-desk clerk	$11.40
Bartender	$8.60
Food-and-beverage server	$7.85

Source: City of Toronto

TAKE 5 FIVE TORONTO
SALARIES

1. **Gordon Nixon, president/CEO Royal Bank of Canada:** $1.4 million base salary, $44.2 million total salary (2008)
2. **Jason Blake, Toronto Maple Leafs forward:** $4.5 million (2008-09 season)
3. **Thomas Gauld, president/CEO Canadian Tire:** $1 million base salary, $5.6 million total salary (2008)
4. **Sheldon Levy, president of Ryerson University:** $312,500 (2007)
5. **Toronto Mayor David Miller:** $163,040 (2008)

WHERE THE MONEY GOES

Toronto CMA households spend an average of $87,168 a year. Here's how it breaks down:

• Income tax	$21,036
• Shelter	$18,688
• Transportation	$10,086
• Food	$7,943
• Insurance/pension payments	$4,688
• Clothing	$4,245
• Household operation	$3,909
• Monetary gifts/contributions	$2,336
• Health care	$1,617
• Education	$1,550
• Personal care	$1,402
• Tobacco and alcohol	$1,392
• Reading material	$295
• Games of chance	$226

Source: Statistics Canada

Did you know. . .

that 23 percent of the workforce in the Toronto CMA is unionized?

TAKE 5 FIVE TORONTO
BILLIONAIRES

1. **David Thomson and family** (media)
2. **Galen Weston and family** (retail)
3. **Bernard (Barry) Sherman** (pharmaceuticals)
4. **Wallace McCain** (food)
5. **Alexander Shnaider** (manufacturing)

Source: Forbes Magazine

GIMME SHELTER

Torontonians had the second highest yearly household expenditures for shelter in the country.

• Yellowknife	$23,192
• **Toronto**	**$18,688**
• Calgary	$16,391
• Vancouver	$15,918
• Edmonton	$14,686
• Halifax	$13,337
• Winnipeg	$11,897
• Montreal	$11,416

Source: Statistics Canada

BUYING A HOUSE

In February of 2009, the average house price in Toronto was $361,361, down from the previous year's $382,048. The figure was about halfway between Fredericton (where the average was $135,834) and Vancouver ($542,641). Toronto prices were above the national average of $281,972, which was down significantly from $310,279 in February of 2008.

AVERAGE HOUSE PRICES IN CANADIAN CITIES

CITY	February 2009	February 2008
Vancouver	$542,641	$623,517
Calgary	$370,198	$415,017
Toronto	**$361,361**	**$382,048**
Yellowknife	$329,491	$314,550
Ottawa	$273,991	$283,199
Hamilton	$265,452	$276,297
Montreal	$250,461	$182,650
Regina	$232,968	$204,459
Halifax	$229,660	$223,579
Winnipeg	$194,558	$183,665
Fredericton	$135,834	$145,347

Source: Canadian Real Estate Association

COST OF A HOUSE (OCT.–DEC. 2008)

	Forest Hill	Scarborough central	Richmond Hill	Cabbagetown
Detached bungalow	none listed	$323,250	$335,750	none listed
Standard two storey	$851,000	$357,750	$360,000	$534,000
Detached Executive two storey	$1,200,000	$425,000	$425,000	$680,000

Did you know. . .

that one of the key trucking destinations in downtown Toronto is the Ontario Food Terminal, just north of the Gardiner by the Humber? The largest in Canada, and the fifth largest in North America, it handles more than 947,000 tons of produce annually.

| Standard condo | $500,000 | $203,000 | | $245,000 | $343,000 |
| Standard townhouse | $940,000 | $235,000 | | $280,000 | $466,000 |

Source: Royal LePage

Bio Edwin Mirvish

Honest Ed Mirvish was the son of poor Lithuanian Jewish immigrants who moved to Toronto in 1923. He was 15 years old when his father died and he quit school to take over the family grocery store. When he died in 2007 at age 92 , he owned the country's biggest bargain store and three swanky theatres. He had also renovated London's Old Vic Theatre, had founded an artist's village and had even been proclaimed "mayor for a day" on his 79th birthday.

Honest Ed's name and personality are synonymous with the gigantic garish discount store that still stands at the corner of Bathurst and Bloor streets. His birthday parties in Mirvish Village were legendary with people lined up for blocks to enjoy the free food, giveaways and live bands.

The secret to Honest Ed's success was to offer lots of cheap merchandise, minimize staff and never allow credit—a practice that had nearly ruined his father's business. He plastered his store with funny slogans (*Honest Ed's an Idiot – His prices are cents-less; Only Our Floors Are Crooked*) and pulled off outlandish publicity stunts, once arranging an in-store roller-skating derby and giving away 30,000 Christmas turkeys through the years.

In 1963 Mirvish bought the Royal Alexandra Theatre to save the Edwardian structure from demolition. He brought blockbuster shows such as *Hair*, *Les Miserables* and *The Lion King* from London and Broadway. In 1993 he built the Princess of Wales Theatre for $22 million.

During Mirvish's funeral in 2007, his store closed and its 22,000 flashing lights were dimmed. South of the border, theatres on Broadway also paid tribute to the showman entrepreneur, dimming their lights for one minute at 8 p.m.

TAKE 5 PAUL GODFREY'S TOP FIVE
POWERBROKERS

Paul Godfrey has had a stellar career in the newspaper business, professional sports management and politics. The life-long Torontonian attended Bathurst Heights Collegiate and graduated from the University of Toronto in 1962 with a bachelor of applied science in chemical engineering. He has served as a councillor, alderman and controller for the City of Toronto, and while serving on Metro Council was elected its chairman for four terms and a record 11 years. Following this political career he moved into the newspaper business, joining the *Toronto Sun* as publisher and CEO. He later became the Sun's president and CEO and headed a management-led buyout that precipitated the formation of Sun Media Corporation. When Rogers Communications Inc. purchased the Toronto Blue Jays Baseball Club in 2000, Godfrey was appointed its president and CEO. He left the Blue Jays in 2008, and on Jan. 1, 2009, became president and CEO of the *National Post*.

1. **Gerry Schwartz:** Gerry Schwartz is the chairman and CEO of Onex and is considered the king of business powerbrokers in Canada. Acquiring and building brand-name companies is what Schwartz and his Onex team does best. Schwartz is the legitimate free enterpriser, having built his company from scratch into a multi-billion dollar empire. Everyone involved in big business in Canada knows Gerry Schwartz. Schwartz and his wife, Heather Reisman, founder of the Indigo bookstores, are truly the number one Canadian business power couple.

2. **John Bitove Jr.:** He is chairman and CEO of XM Canada and chairman and CEO of Priszm Canadian Income Fund (owner and operator of 479 KFC, Pizza Hut and Taco Bell restaurants in Canada). In 1993, Bitove founded the Toronto Raptors Basketball Club. Bitove recently entered the wireless field as chairman and CEO of DAVE Wireless. Bitove is young, positively aggressive, a visionary and has the knowledge and people skills necessary to make a success of anything he touches.

3. **Dale Lastman:** Dale Lastman is co-chair of Goodmans law firm. He is a Director of Maple Leaf Sports & Entertainment Ltd., RioCan REIT and Roots Canada Ltd., and is an alternate NHL governor to the league for the Toronto Maple Leafs. He was a recipient of "Canada's Top 40 Under 40" in 1995 and is a lecturer in securities law at Osgoode Hall Law School. He is one of the best securities lawyers in Canada. Many business leaders contemplating a major acquisition, merger or takeover want Lastman to coordinate and advise on the strategy of the deal. He is smart, honest, and direct and always seems to find the path to success. Lastman often takes on tasks that appear impossible to solve and brings warring opponents together to create a win/win situation.

4. **Larry Tanenbaum:** The quiet and behind-the-scenes chairman of Kilmer Capital Partners Limited and chairman and CEO of KVN is one of the true powerbrokers in Canada. He avoids the spotlight whenever possible and is the chairman of the board of Maple Leaf Sports and Entertainment (owner of the NHL Maple Leafs and NBA Toronto Raptors). Tanenbaum is a great deal maker. He is smart but modest, goal-oriented but laid back. His multi-faceted company includes construction operation with operating divisions and subsidiaries covering road building and paving, ready-mix concrete, heavy construction, trucking and pipe manufacturing. Tanenbaum spends considerable time and energy in the charitable sector, helping to build the community by strengthening the bonds between government and numerous worthwhile and needy causes.

5. **Ontario Teachers' Pension Plan Board:** The Ontario Teachers' Pension Plan was not identified as a major power broker until the mid-1990s. Their 50-person investment team includes some of the smartest and shrewdest people in Canada. They are virtually faceless to the public, but have a major say in almost everything they touch. They have been successful investors in Shoppers' Drug Mart, Cadillac Fairview, Sun Media, and Maple Leaf Sports and Entertainment, to mention just a few.

RENTING

Toronto is a city of renters. It has almost half-a-million rental units and average rents are the highest in the country, just edging out Calgary and Vancouver. But it's not as hard to find a place in T.O. as it is in Vancouver, Regina, Winnipeg, Ottawa and Saskatoon.

- Percentage of Torontonians who rent: 49
- Average monthly rent: $900 (one bedroom)
- Average monthly rent: $1,061 (two bedrooms)
- Average vacancy rate in Toronto in October 2008: 2 percent

Source: City of Toronto, Metro Tenants Association

BUILDING-PERMIT VALUES (2008)

- Toronto: $12.24 billion
- Vancouver: $5.58 billion
- Montreal: $6.4 billion
- Calgary: $4.7 billion
- Ottawa/Gatineau (Quebec): $2.4 billion
- Ottawa/Gatineau (Ontario): $1.8 billion

Source: Statistics Canada

RENTS IN SELECTED CANADIAN CITIES

City	One bedroom	Two bedrooms
Toronto	$900	$1,061
Calgary	$897	$1,089
Vancouver	$846	$1,084
Ottawa	$798	$961
Edmonton	$784	$958
Kingston	$701	$856
Halifax	$659	$815
Montreal	$581	$647
Winnipeg	$578	$740
Saskatoon	$564	$693

Source: Canada Mortgage and Housing Corporation

APARTMENT VACANCY RATES IN CANADIAN CITIES

City	Vacancy rate (October 2008)
Vancouver	0.5 percent
Regina	0.5 percent
Winnipeg	1.0 percent
Ottawa	1.4 percent
Saskatoon	1.9 percent
Toronto	**2.0 percent**
Calgary	2.1 percent
Montreal	2.4 percent
Halifax	3.4 percent

Source: Canada Mortgage and Housing Corporation.

THE TORONTO COMMUTE

Although many Torontonians are crazy about their cars, and the city is not without its traffic headaches, auto use is actually moderate compared to other places in Canada. Slightly more than one-fifth of those living in the Toronto CMA—and almost one-third, if just city residents are counted—use public transit to get to work; those are the highest numbers for any major CMA that Statistics Canada tracks. By contrast, only 2.4 percent of workers in Saguenay, Que., use public transit, the lowest rate in the country. Ridership is higher in larger CMAs: 21.4 percent of workers in Montreal use public transit, as do 16.5 percent of workers in Vancouver and 15.6 percent in Calgary.

HOW TORONTONIANS GET TO WORK (TORONTO CMA)

- 71.1 percent drive or carpool
- 22.2 percent use public transit
- 4.8 percent walk
- 1 percent bicycles
- 0.9 percent use another form of transportation

Source: Statistics Canada

NO PARKING

The City of Toronto oversees 20,000 off-street parking spaces in 180 facilities, including 22 parking garages, and 18,000 on-street parking spaces with either meters or pay-and-display kiosks. The median cost for monthly parking was $290 in 2008, well up from the national average of $211.94 and about the same as the median rate in Montreal, but low compared to Calgary's $428.

WHAT KIND OF JOBS TORONTONIANS HAVE

- Office: 46.3 percent
- Institutional (government): 16 percent
- Retail: 11.7 percent
- Service: 11.5 percent
- Manufacturing: 11.4 percent

EMPLOYMENT BY THE NUMBERS

The 2007 employment figures for the Toronto CMA broke into these sectors:

- Total: 2,865,510
- Manufacturing: 404,340
- Retail trade: 338,750
- Professional, scientific and technical services: 274,340
- Health care and social assistance: 243,030
- Finance and insurance: 213,280
- Educational services: 197,080
- Construction: 168,680
- Accommodations and food services: 157,920
- Transportation and warehousing: 136,700
- Administrative and support, waste management and remediation: 132,940
- Wholesale trade: 125,860
- Other services (except public administration): 115,790
- Information and cultural industries: 97,140
- Public administration: 91,540
- Real estate and rental leasing: 72,780
- Arts, entertainment and recreation: 66,620
- Utilities: 15,550
- Agriculture, forestry, fishing and hunting: 9,190
- Minerals and oil and gas extraction: 2,980

Source: City of Toronto

THE LARGE AND THE SMALL OF IT

No. of Employees	Percentage of Toronto Businesses
1–4	56.1 percent
5–9	19.2 percent
10–19	11.1 percent
20–59	8 percent
50–99	3 percent
100–199	1.5 percent
200–999	1 percent
1,000+	0.1 percent

Source: City of Toronto

First Baron of the Fleet

What is most fascinating about fortunes lost and made is how often they turn on an unpredictable stroke of good luck—or the combination of good luck plus opportunity recognized and seized. In the case of Roy Thomson, he was hawking radios in northern Ontario and needed to give his potential buyers something to listen to. He bought a transmitter and receiver for just over $200, and CFCH was in business.

Three years later Thomson bought the Timmins Daily Press for another $200. When he died in 1976, his empire had grown in value to $750 million. His son Kenneth, and now grandson David, increased the family's personal wealth to $25.4 billion, making the Thomsons one of the richest families in the world, with a wealth more than double that of any other family in the country.

The son of a Toronto barber, Roy Thomson was famously thrifty, and despite being awarded a Lordship, Baron of Fleet, he eschewed pomp and circumstance. He recognized as early as 1964 that managing a family fortune into the second and third generation would be markedly different than his own rise. The business is all tied up in trusts, he told the national media, adding

SELF-EMPLOYMENT

Working for yourself is an increasingly popular option in Toronto. A total of 458,800 people, or 16 percent of the Toronto CMA workforce, were self-employed in 2007, an increase of 70.3 percent over 15 years ago. Nationwide, 2,653,500 people were self-employed as of November 2008.

Source: City of Toronto, Statistics Canada

TRANSPORTATION INFRASTRUCTURE

Although the once the engine of Toronto's prosperity, waterfront-based manufacturing has yielded prominence to service-based industry, but outlying manufacturing is still served by well-established networks

that even if his family wanted to shrug off responsibilities, they would not be able to do so.

Thomson's son Kenneth attended Upper Canada College, as did Kenneth's son David. They would arrive in a chauffeur-driven car. The life of the barber's son was really more part of family lore than practice. The Thomsons were now inextricably linked to wealth with a single mandate: make their fortune even larger.

Great cities always benefit from the presence of billionaires, and Toronto has benefited from the Thomsons as New York City did from the Rockefellers. One of the premier arts venues in the city is Roy Thomson Hall, so named because of the Thomson family's generous donation. Before his death, Ken Thomson had donated more than 2,000 pieces of art to the Art Gallery of Ontario; he also provided $50 million in capital funding for the recent AGO expansion, plus $20 million more in endowment funding.

Roy Thomson's roots go back to the first settlers of Scarborough, and the family has remained staunch Toronto loyalists ever since. The question is, what mark will the third generation make on their city?

of high-volume air, road, rail and water-transport facilities. Toronto-based businesses find it relatively easy to export $70 billion in goods and services annually, right around the world, and the city is within a day's drive for 30 million people.

AIR

Toronto's two airports are Lester B. Pearson International—Canada's busiest, just west of the city—and Toronto City Centre Airport at the western end of the Toronto Islands, often referred to as the Island Airport.

Pearson ranks as the fourth-largest international airport in North America and is indispensable to Toronto's import/export activities and executive travel. Often called "Canada's gateway to the world," it has direct flights to 27 Canadian destinations, 42 American locations and 84 international cities, and it sends more flights to the U.S. than any other airport in the world. In 2007 it handled 31.5 million people on 79 airlines.

Pearson is just as busy and critical to the economy on the cargo front. In 2006 alone it handled more than half a million metric tonnes, or 45 percent of all air cargo in Canada—a volume worth $31.7 billion—and with 1.2 million square feet of warehouse space it can easily double this amount. Pearson ranks in the world's top 30 airports for its cargo capacity and facilities, including heavyweight cargo runways and more than 240 truck loading doors; almost 50 large freight-forwarding companies nearby handle the flow of goods.

The much smaller Island Airport is only minutes from downtown; it's accessible by ferry or water taxi and used mainly for short-haul business travel, mostly within Canada. It has about 120,000 landings and takeoffs a year, about half as many as in its 1960s heydays.

PORT

While not as critical to the city's economic output as it once was, the Port of Toronto is still a major link on the 3,747 km St. Lawrence Seaway and connects the city to the world by water. In 2007, some 2.07 million tonnes of cargo passed through the harbour, a volume that made it Canada's seventh-busiest port but still put it well behind the big three of Vancouver, Montreal and Halifax. With easy links to rail and truck lines, the harbour funnels cargo to and from Ontario, northwest Quebec, upstate New York and Ohio and generates an estimated $422 million in port-related business. Sugar, salt and cement are the top three bulk cargos.

The commercial port area covers 50 acres and has three kilometres of frontage along the eastern end of the harbour. The Toronto Port Authority oversees commercial shipping activities from marine termi-

TAKE *5* FIVE KEY EMPLOYMENT
SECTORS IN TORONTO

1. **Financial services:** Toronto is the largest banking and finance centre in Canada and the third largest in North America. It's home to Canada's five largest banks and six of its top insurance companies, 50 foreign bank subsidiaries and 112 securities businesses, not to mention the TSX.

2. **Business services:** Law and accounting firms, advertising and marketing agencies, human resources, management, technical and design consultancies and customer care centres—together these employ some 300,000 people, and the sector is growing at the rate of six percent a year.

3. **Information and communication technology:** With $20 billion in annual revenues, Toronto's ICT sector is the largest in Canada and third largest in North America. In 2004 the city boasted 1,685 companies with 75,000 employees, while in the GTA numbers were 3,362 companies and 148,000 employees.

4. **Food-and-beverage services:** More than 50,000 employees staff more than 2,000 food-and-beverage manufacturers, with annual sales exceeding $17 billion. Major players include Weston Bakeries and the Canadian branches of Cadbury, Schweppes, Kraft, Nestlé, Unilever and Campbell's Soup.

5. **Aerospace:** More than 200 aerospace firms in the Toronto area employ upward of 20,000 people and generate more than $6 billion annually in sales of products and services. The big companies include Bombardier, Pratt & Whitney, Magellan and Honeywell.

nals No. 51 and No. 52 and also owns and operates the Island Airport and the outer-harbour marina. It opened an international terminal in 2005 to service visiting cruise ships.

RAIL

In Ontario, all tracks lead to Toronto's Union Station, Canada's biggest and busiest passenger transportation facility. The station is a hub for commuter GO train, passenger and freight trains, as well as the subway, handling 35 million people and 55,000 passenger trains a year.

TAKE 5 KEVIN O'LEARY'S FIVE
UNIQUELY TORONTO INNOVATIONS

Kevin O'Leary received an honours bachelor's degree in environmental studies and psychology from the University of Waterloo and an MBA from the University of Western Ontario. After he graduated, he became a founding partner in Special Event Television. He co-founded SoftKey Software Products in Toronto, and in 1995 SoftKey acquired the first of six companies, making it the world leader in the development of educational, reference and home-productivity software with annual sales of over $800 million, 2,000 employees and subsidiaries in 15 countries. In 1996 SoftKey became The Learning Company, and three years later The Mattel Toy Company acquired The Learning Company for $4.2 billion. O'Leary is the chairman of O'Leary Funds and the manager of the publicly traded O'Leary Global Equity Income and O'Leary Global Infrastructure Fund. He is a frequent cohost on the Business News Network and one of the dragons on CBC's venture capital reality TV program *Dragon's Den*.

1. **Energy Savings Income Fund:** Publicly traded income trust providing more than one million residential, small to mid-size commercial and small industrial customers with the peace of mind that comes from knowing that they are protected from energy-price volatility by offering access to fixed utility pricing.

GO trains, which alone carry 100,000 to 150,000 daily, have just been subsumed by a new regional people carrier called Metrolinx. Union really is "grand central" when it comes to moving commuters into and out of the downtown core.

Freight-rail functions, once also based along the waterfront, have now mostly moved north from the lakefront. CN and CPR lines link Toronto with 33,000 km of railway lines in North America and have been updated with multi-modal facilities, which allow roads to handle the short-haul shipping and rail and ship to do the long-distance work.

2. **407 ETR:** First Canadian public/private endeavour for building out infrastructure. It's the world's first all-electronic open-access toll highway. With 530 million total trips under its belt since 1997, it's one of the largest construction projects in Canadian history and remains one of the world's most modern highway systems.

3. **Income trusts:** An innovative way to raise funds for resource-based companies. These trusts that hold income-producing assets have allowed the investor to participate in the income and capital based on the cash flows of the underlying business. They have offered consistent monthly double-digit cash flow to the investor for over 15 years, which became especially attractive when cash yields on bonds were low.

4. **Toronto Maple Leafs:** One of the most profitable and valuable sports entertainment franchises in the NHL, at $488 million in 2008, despite not having won the Stanley Cup in more than 40 years.

5. **Trattoria Sotto Sotto restaurant (Yorkville):** Best place in Canada for a power dinner or to conduct a business deal. Always consistent in food quality, service and wine selection and packed every day of the week.

ROAD

Toronto's network of multi-lane highways is indispensable to the flow of commuter and freight traffic. The main east-west corridor above downtown is Highway 401, which handles about 300,000 vehicles every weekday. Part of the Trans-Canada Highway, the 401 is the major connecting highway between Montreal and Toronto and to and from points west. Up to 18 lanes wide in some parts of the city, it is among the world's widest highways, and the overpass at Yonge Street has the world's busiest multi-structure bridge. Highways 400 and 404 extend the road links north out of Toronto.

TRADE

Ontario's trade partners by percentage of export business:

- United States   86.5 percent
- United Kingdom   3.2 percent
- Rest of European Union 2.9 percent
- China   0.82 percent

LEADING CANADIAN CITIES FOR HEAD OFFICE EMPLOYMENT

Toronto, Montreal, Calgary and Vancouver account for the lion's share, at 73 percent, of head office employment in Canada, with Toronto leading the way:

- **Toronto**   **59,163 (34 percent)**
- Montreal   36,893 (21 percent)
- Calgary   19,428 (11 percent)
- Vancouver   11,938 (7 percent)
- Winnipeg   6,890 or (4 percent)

Source: Statistics Canada

OFFICE SPACE

	Millions of square feet	Vacancy rate	Class A net rental ($psf)
Toronto	74.6	4.9 percent	$24.74
Montreal	42.2	5.7 percent	$21.30

Calgary	33.1	5.2 percent	$46.27
Vancouver	21.8	3.1 percent	$35.33
Ottawa	22.6	2.2 percent	$24.08
Edmonton	13.9	5.5 percent	$26.78
Winnipeg	7.2	5.9 percent	$15.56
Halifax	4.5	4.3 percent	$18.60

Source: City of Toronto

FOREIGN-OFFICE RENTAL COSTS PER SQUARE FOOT

London, England	$212
Tokyo, Japan	$145.68
Manhattan, U.S.	$62
Asuncion, Paraguay	$10.03

Source: Monster.ca

Weblinks

Toronto Board of Trade
www.bot.com/sub/HomePages/PublicHomePage.asp
News and views from Canada's largest chamber of commerce.

Canada's Biggest City and its $$$
www.tedco.ca
Details of the city's business scene from the Toronto Economic Development Corporation.

Doing Business in Toronto
www.toronto.ca/business/index.htm
Want to launch or expand a business in Toronto or find work? This official City of Toronto site is a good place to start your planning.

Canadian Business Hall of Fame
www.cbhof.org
An impressive array of Canadian tycoons, many of whom were born, lived or worked in Toronto.

Then and Now

The initial stimulus for Toronto's rise to prominence had more to do with a strategic location—further removed from the increasingly long reach of America than Upper Canada's previous capital—than its intrinsic merits, pleasant and promising as they were. Once it was established as the centre of Upper Canada, however, the machinery of government ensured both the town's survival and its importance.

The population increased slowly at first but by the mid-1800s was expanding rapidly. Toronto also added great chunks to its numbers and area over the years by annexing adjacent towns and villages. The character of its population changed significantly as the decades passed, at first slowly, from thoroughly British with an Irish Catholic supporting class, and through the 1900s much more swiftly, with the arrival of a host of immigrant groups.

Today Toronto is a truly cosmopolitan city, with large communities of people hailing from Asia, the Middle East, North Africa and the Americas. For this and many other reasons, the changes over the last century have been immense, and the unknown future will be shaped by the efforts of the new mix of international Torontonians.

POPULATION

The leaps in population growth have some key watermarks. The most recent spike occurred with the 1998 amalgamation that created the megacity.

1814: 720
1834: 9,254
1851: 30, 775
1876: 68,000
1901: 208, 040

TAKE 5 FIVE THEN-AND-NOW
PRICE HIKES

1. **At the movies:** The first moving picture was shown in Toronto in 1896 at M.S. Robinson's Musée at 10 cents a ticket. Today prices vary by theatre and cost anywhere from $10 to $15 per adult.

2. **At the theatre:** The Winter Garden Theatre opened in 1914; tickets for a show cost 25 to 50 cents. Today you might get a special $20 ticket deal at Mirvish.com, but standard prices reach as high as $200 for a good seat on a weekend night.

3. **For medical aid:** The 1839 doctors' rates at the York General Hospital included:
- Daytime medical opinion/visit inside the city: 5 shillings ($1.25)
- Nighttime medical opinion/visit inside the city: £1 ($5)
- Bleeding or tooth extraction: visit charge, plus 2 shillings 6 pence
- Consultation: £1 ($5)

4. **At the King Eddie:** When Elizabeth Taylor and Richard Burton stayed at the King Edward Hotel in 1964, the cost was $65 per day for a suite. In the spring of 2009, one night cost between $286 and $451, plus tax (afternoon high tea included).

5. **To see the Leafs Play:** When the Gardens opened in 1931, the top-price ticket was $2.75. The 2009 top price is $401.51. The cheapest seats are $44.61.

1941: 667, 457
1961: 672, 407   Metro – 1,358,028
1981: 599, 217   Metro – 2,137,395
1996: 653,734   Metro – 2,385,421
2001: 2,481,494   (post-amalgamation)
2006: 2,503,281

WAGES

In 1796 an unskilled labourer in York earned $1 a day, and a skilled carpenter would make $2. Government jobs were the best positions, and a Justice of the King's Bench earned about $3,750 a year in the early 1800s. When T.E. Eaton opened his Yonge Street store in 1869, his staff was paid $4 per day (female) or $6–8 (male), and the delivery boy made $1 a day.

In a high-minded move in 1893, Toronto brought in a fair wage policy to ensure that all city contractors paid union rates. The policy has since expanded to include other workers and suppliers, and it cover hours of work and health and safety issues. Today any firm bidding on a city tender must comply with its fair wage policy, which covers both salaries and benefits.

THE CHEQUE IS IN THE MAIL

In 1809 mail between York and Quebec City took 19 days to arrive. With no residential mail delivery, residents would often compose their mail right in the post office; the postmaster would also read mail for the illiterate.

The City of Toronto had four post offices when it incorporated in 1834; the fourth was at 260 Adelaide St. East, which was then Duke Street. It rented 204 mailboxes and was open 11 hours a day, Monday to Saturday, and an hour on Sunday for churchgoers. In the 1830s, mail to England could take as much as two months to arrive. Today the Adelaide East post office is both functional and a museum. Boxes can be rented, the writing room with its fireplace can still be used and letters can be sent with a reproduction of an 1834 stamp.

THE GREAT FIRE OF 1904

The Great Fire of 1904 started in Toronto's wholesale district. Reduced to rubble was the area roughly between Yonge and Bay, from Melinda to the Esplanade, so much of the downtown. The conflagration put more than 5,000 workers out of work permanently or temporarily, and losses reached $10 million (1904 dollars).

The events of April 19, 1904:

TAKE 5 BRUCE BELL'S FIVE FAVOURITE ROOMS IN TORONTO

The city's unofficial historian, Bruce Bell writes a popular monthly column on the history of Toronto for *The Bulletin*, Canada's largest community newspaper, and has penned two history books about the city. He is the official historian of St. Lawrence Hall and Market and the honourary historian for two Toronto heritage buildings: The Hockey Hall of Fame and Toronto Police Services 51 Division. His "history project" marks historical sites with bronze plaques.

1. **The Grand Ballroom of St. Lawrence Hall (157 King St. East):** Architect William Thomas completed St. Lawrence Hall in 1851, and for the next 25 years it was Toronto's pre-eminent concert hall. One of the first people to give a talk in the newly opened Great Hall on April 1, 1851, was renowned abolitionist Frederick Douglass. This great ballroom, with its massive gas-lit chandelier, was once home to the National Ballet of Canada and is still in use today.

2. **Sovereign Room at the King Edward Hotel (37 King St. East):** The King Edward Hotel made a splash when it opened in 1903, with its sweeping parlours and elegantly appointed lounges. It has been updated over the years, but one grand room remains almost untouched by time: the Sovereign Ballroom, formerly the Victorian Dining Room, a stunning example of Edwardian design at its best.

- 8:04 p.m.: Fire is spotted in the E & S Currie Building on Wellington by a watchman. It spreads quickly; soon both sides of Bay and Wellington are burning.
- 9 p.m.: Every firefighter in the city is on the scene. The mayor telegraphs SOSs and firefighters arrive through the night from as far away as Niagara Falls, Buffalo, London and Peterborough.
- 11 p.m.: The fire stops moving north but sweeps along Front toward Yonge and south to the Esplanade.

3. **Banking Hall of Commerce Court (25 King St. East):** Regarded as a national treasure, the former banking hall of the Bank of Commerce, with its vaulted ceiling of gold leaf and hand-painted murals, can hold its own alongside any European cathedral. Opened in 1929, the site is the head office for the Canadian Imperial Bank of Commerce.

4. **The Imperial Room at the Fairmont Royal York Hotel (100 Front St. West):** When the Royal York Hotel opened, Torontonians gasped at its sheer size: it had a thousand guest rooms, a palatial lobby, a massive concert hall and a luxurious supper club in which to wine, dine and dance the night away. The Imperial Room was the last of the great supper clubs. Ella Fitzgerald, Tony Bennett and Duke Ellington all entertained here, while guests dined in one of the most sumptuous rooms in Canada.

5. **The Banking Hall of the Toronto Dominion Centre (55 King St. West):** A modern masterpiece that is just as stunning today as it was when it opened in 1966, the banking hall of the TD Centre by Mies van der Rohe carried Toronto out of its post-war "dull drums" and brought new vitality to the city. Van der Rohe's vision included placing fresh-cut yellow daisies in clear, round, glass vases on all four corners of the tellers' counter in the main-floor banking hall, as well as on the CEO's desk 54 storeys above, the type of timeless detail and art for which he was famous.

- 4:30 a.m.: The main fire is finally under control.
- Following days: Small fires continue to break out; the ruins smolder for a couple of weeks.

The cause of the 1904 fire is still unknown, although early reports suggested either faulty wiring or a stove left burning at the end of the workday.

HOLD THE LINE

The first telephones rang in Toronto in 1877, thanks to Dr. A.M. Rosebrough, a friend of the Alexander Graham Bell family. In 1878 Rosebrough and two partners founded the Telephone Despatch Company and published a telephone booklet a year later for 56 subscribers. The Bell Telephone Company of Canada bought the company in 1881. Subscribers joined quickly; 400 in 1881 grew to 3,400 by 1891.

The city's exchanges eventually had a name plus four digits; early names were MAin, NOrth and BEach. When Foster Hewitt broadcast his first Maple Leafs hockey game in 1923, the link from his studio at the Mutual Street arena to the *Toronto Star's* radio station CFCA was by phone, and the broadcast featured operators occasionally breaking in to ask, "Number please?" All-digit dialing finally arrived in Toronto in the early 1960s.

COST OF GETTING AROUND

Toronto has an intermittent relationship with toll roads. In the 1800s, they were spread over the city and operated both publicly and privately. In 1865, for example, four streets—the "York Roads" or Yonge, Dundas, Kingston Road and Lakeshore Road—were in private hands. By 1875 typical toll rates were seven cents for a vehicle with one horse/beast, 10 cents if there were two horses but only four cents for beast and rider. These early tollgates were abolished in 1896.

Today there's a toll on Highway 407, north of the city, and debate recurs about introducing more, as London, England, has done to reduce downtown traffic congestion. A trip across the top of the city spanning 33.8 km costs slightly less than $7 during morning rush hour.

What about crossing water? In the 1800s, passengers and goods had to pay to cross the Humber or Credit rivers by ferry. In 1810 these fares were decreased; it became one pence for a hog, 2.3 for a passenger, five if he or she was on a horse and more for carriages. Free bridges eventually replaced the ferries, although today you still have to pay to take a boat to the Toronto Islands. The cost varies for water taxis; the public ferry will take an adult for $6.50 and a child for $3, while infants under two are free.

Stork Derby

In October of 1926, a quirky Canadian lawyer, well-known for his off-the-wall sense of humor, died suddenly of a heart attack. As eccentric in death as he had been in life, the last will and testament of Charles Vance Millar generated a decade of excitement for mothers living in Toronto.

In a bizarre clause, Millar left a huge portion of his considerable fortune to the Toronto woman who would deliver the most babies in the decade following his death. Of course Millar could not have known that the world was about to be plunged into recession when he started his baby race, dubbed the "stork derby." But when times got hard, Toronto women took the contest seriously; after all, the $750,000 dollars up for grabs was no small sum, especially in the Dirty Thirties.

The 10-year contest was marked by political infighting and court challenges. One contestant, Pauline Clarke, gave the contest her best shot, bearing 10 children in 10 years. The fact that her children had different fathers did not go over well in the morally conservative city, however, and she was disqualified. Another woman, Lillian Kenney, was disqualified because several of her 12 children died in childbirth and were not counted in her total. The prize ended up being split between four women who had each given birth to 10 children during the decade. Kenney and Clarke were given $12,500 for what the committee called their "effort."

EDUCATION

The University of Toronto, Upper Canada's first university, was chartered as King's College in 1827, although its first class of 26 students didn't attend the school's single building until 1843. Most had come from Upper Canada College, the only school with high enough standards to qualify its students. Anglican-affiliated at first, it became a secular institution in 1849, changing its name to the University of Toronto.

Today more than 63,000 students pursue degrees on U of T's three campuses: St. George, Scarborough and Mississauga. The university is also affiliated with 10 teaching hospitals and several other research

Bio Alexander Wood

In 1793 Alexander Wood, an ambitious 21-year-old, set out first for Kingston, moving later to York to establish himself there as a leading merchant. He quickly connected with the powerful elite; by 1798 Wood was made a lieutenant in the York militia, in 1800 he was appointed magistrate and in 1805 he became a commissioner for the Court of Requests.

In 1810 Wood took a terrible risk when he told a number of young men a fictional story: that a woman had been raped but managed to scrape her attacker's genitals, and as a result he was duty-bound to inspect their genitals. Word quickly spread and the scandal could not be ignored. One resident joker referred to him as Inspector General of Private Accounts.

In the end, his friend Judge Powell asked Wood if the story was true. Wood confessed, and Powell agreed to make the evidence go away on the condition that Wood leave Upper Canada. Two years after leaving, however, he returned, resuming all of his previous occupations, including that of magistrate.

Although the sordid affair would come up again when Chief Justice Powell attempted to block his appointment to the commission to investigate war claims in 1823, Wood, who still had powerful allies, would win the day. When he died in 1844, the British Colonist called him one of Toronto's "most respected inhabitants."

facilities and institutes, and the downtown campus covers several city blocks. Females were not accepted at U of T until 1884; today 56 percent of students are women. The University of Toronto is the 15th-largest employer in the Greater Toronto Area, and its economic impact is estimated at almost $6 billion.

SIMCOE DAY

The first Monday in August may be known to other Canadians, and even to most Torontonians, as the August civic holiday, but in Toronto it is officially called Simcoe Day. It is a municipal holiday in the city but doesn't have statutory status. The tradition dates to 1869, when the city decided it needed a midsummer "day of recreation." Two years later the British House of Commons established the bank holiday, which gave Anglo Toronto a suitable bandwagon upon which to hop. In 1875 Toronto council declared the first Monday in August a civic holiday, and in 1968 it became Simcoe Day.

RIOTS

The first Jubilee Riot happened on Sept. 26, 1875. Marching Roman Catholics, directed by the Archbishop to conduct pilgrimages following the pope's declaration of a Jubilee year, were met by angry Orangemen known as Little Britons. Two weeks later, on Oct. 3, the two groups of between 8,000 and 20,000 rioters clashed again, resulting in hundreds of injuries to police officers and members of the angry crowds.

Did you know. . .

that in 1816 it took four days to reach Niagara Falls by stagecoach? Today it takes about an hour and a half by car, depending on traffic.

CHRISTIE PITS RIOT

The five-hour Christie Pits Riot, which occurred on Aug. 16, 1933, in what was then known as Willowvale Park, was one of the ugliest in Toronto's history. At the time, despite newspaper articles that described Nazi atrocities against Jews in Germany, Toronto anti-Semites began banding together. A junior softball tournament between the non-Jewish St. Peter's team and the all-Jewish Harbord Playground team was tailor-made for the bigots to stir up trouble.

The Harbord Playground team won the first game in spite of racial taunts. At the second game, when St. Peter's supporters raised a sheet painted with a black swastika, a group of Jewish supporters moved in to tear it down. A fight ensued, and soon thousands of spectators had joined in; many area residents rushed out armed with bats, pipes and sticks to join the fray. To restore order, Toronto police closed the park. Miraculously, no one was killed, and such large-scale violence was never repeated.

TAKE 5 FIVE PEOPLE WHO INSPIRED TORONTO STREET NAMES

1. **King Street:** George III was king when Governor-General Simcoe developed York; Charlotte Street is named for his queen.
2. **Hazelton Avenue:** Joseph Hazelton came to Toronto in 1850 and ran one of the city's first horse-drawn cab companies.
3. **Lisgar Street:** Sir John Young, aka Lord Lisgar, was Canada's second governor-general.
4. **Bloor Street:** Joseph Bloor was a land developer in the 1880s.
5. **The Gardiner Expressway:** The first chairman of the Metro level of government was Frederick Golden "Big Daddy" Gardiner (1895–1983); technically, it's the F.G. Gardiner Expressway.

Casa Loma

The fabulous wealth of the Robber Barons south of the border had a few parallel stories among Toronto's elite. Although our ties were to Mother Britannia, the desire for conspicuous consumption was a shared North American preoccupation.

Sir Henry Pellatt belonged to that ruling Toronto establishment. He studied at Upper Canada College, leaving early to join his father's brokerage firm. For a while, everything the younger Pellatt touched seemed to turn to gold. He founded the Toronto Electric Light Company in 1883, which enjoyed a monopoly on supplying street lighting to the city. He also invested heavily in the Northwest Land Company and the Canadian Pacific Railway, as well as national power companies.

By the turn of the century, Pellatt was chairman of 21 companies and had an estimated fortune of $17 million. Knighted in 1905, Sir Henry was soon ready to take his place as head of the Toronto establishment, building what would be at that time the largest estate in North America.

The plans were drawn in 1911. Located on Austin Terrace, Casa Loma had 98 rooms and an elevator, secret passages and an 800-foot tunnel connecting the castle to the stables. In a city already known for its conservatism, it was a show of opulence not seen before or since.

Unfortunately for Pellatt, his investing luck headed south soon afterward. Ownership of the electrical utility changed from private to public, and land speculation (he believed wealthy Torontonians would want to build near Casa Loma) was hampered by a wartime economy that saw Canadians preferring to save rather than spend.

Less than 10 years after the Pellats moved in they were bankrupt, forced to sell their furnishings and valuable artwork at a fifth of their cost and leave their palatial home. Lady Pellat cracked under the strain, dying within a year. When Sir Henry died in 1939, thousands of Torontonians crowded the streets to get a glimpse of the man who had the audacity to think he could build a castle on the hill.

DEPRESSION FIGURES

- In 1933 the average per capita income in Ontario was $310, down from $549 in 1928–29.
- Building permits, a sign of a city's vibrancy, were worth $51 million to Toronto in 1928 but fell to $30 million in 1930 and a little more than $4 million in 1933.
- Manufacturing jobs decreased by 26,000, a loss of a quarter of the city's pre-Depression workforce.
- Transients from rural areas flocked to Toronto looking for work; 23,000 of the 44,000 single men who applied for relief in the city between 1931 and 1936 were from out of town.

TAKE 5 FIVE TORONTO
INVENTIONS

1. **Pablum:** This now ubiquitous, vitamin-heavy baby food was developed by Dr. Frederick Tisdall and Dr. Theodore Drake for young patients at Toronto's Hospital for Sick Children in the early 1930s. It became commercially available in 1931.

2. **Buckley's cough syrup:** The notoriously awful-tasting cough syrup was invented by Toronto pharmacist William Knapp Buckley shortly after the end of World War I.

3. **Ginger ale:** Toronto pharmacist and chemist John McClaughlin invented the fizzy refreshment in the early 1900s and called it Canada Dry Pale Ginger Ale.

4. **Plug-in radios:** Edward "Ted" Rogers Sr. invented the world's first alternating current (AC) radio tube in 1925. It allowed listeners simply to plug a radio into a wall socket instead of using expensive batteries.

5. **Table hockey:** The first mechanical table hockey game was invented in Toronto by Donald Munro in the late 1930s. The Munro Standard model was listed in the 1939–40 Eaton's catalogue at $4.95.

- By 1934 nearly 120,000 unemployed people in the city were on relief.

As a demonstration of his commitment to cost cutting, Ontario Premier Mitch Hepburn held a bizarre sell-off in 1934 in Toronto's Varsity Stadium when he put 87 vehicles from the previous Conservative government on the auction block. The 8,000 people in attendance spent $34,000.

ALL THE LIVE LONG DAY

1852: The Grand Trunk Railway Company forms in order to build a line between Toronto and Montreal.

1853: The first steam train leaves Toronto from a wooden shed on Front Street opposite the Queen's Hotel. Destination: Aurora.

1855: A 153 km portage line is completed between Toronto and Collingwood.

1856: The Grand Trunk Railway completes its Toronto-to-Sarnia line in July and its Toronto-to-Montreal line in October.

1872: The first Union Station is built on Front Street between York and Simcoe streets.

1911: Union Station has 40,000 passengers and more than 130 trains daily.

1926: The first locomotive powered by oil and electricity pulls into Toronto from Montreal. Toronto Mayor Sam McBride welcomes Montreal Mayor Camillien Houde and other dignitaries.

1927: A new Beaux-Arts-style Union Station opens.

1967: GO Transit begins operating out of Union Station with a train to Oakville.

2007: Toronto city council accepts redevelopment plans for Union Station that will increase capacity and economic opportunity while maintaining the area's historic integrity.

Today: Union Station is the busiest transit hub in Canada, handling 250,000 passengers a day, 65 million annually; that's twice as many people as Pearson International Airport.

GOING MOBILE

In 1902 "Muddy York" was still an apt name for Toronto. Despite the city's 64 km of asphalt pavement, plus another 100 km or so laid from cedar blocks, brick or gravel, most of its 410 km of streets were still dirt or, when it rained, mud. Vehicle traffic on those mean streets was all horse-powered until 1893, when Toronto's (and Canada's) first electric car appeared running on streetcar lines. It was followed in 1898 by the city's first internal-combustion vehicle.

It hasn't all been happy motoring since then. The first car/pedestrian fatality occurred in 1907. Today, according to the Toronto Collision Clock, the city's streets produce a fender-bender every 9.8 minutes, a personal injury every 9.2 hours and a death every 6.4 days.

In 1875 the T. Eaton Company was delivering goods by horse and wagon. By 1919 it had 200 wagons, 310 horses and 66 motor-trucks of varying sizes. Toronto's first motorized taxis appeared in 1909. De Luxe Cab Ltd., established in 1926, and nine other cab companies merged in 1949 to form Diamond Taxi, which is still in business. Imperial Oil opened the first gas station in 1914. Gasoline was 22.5 cents a gallon then; the first provincial fuel tax appeared in 1925. Toronto's first auto show was held in 1904 and soon became an annual attraction. The 2008 event, now the Canadian International Auto Show, drew more than 300,000 visitors.

PUBLIC TRANSPORTATION

1849: The Williams Omni Bus Line provides the city's first public transit, horse-drawn stagecoaches, between St. Lawrence Market and Yorkville. The fare is sixpence.

1861: The privately owned Toronto Street Railway Company wins the franchise for the city's first street railway; it provides horse-drawn streetcars in summer and horse-drawn sleighs in winter.

1892: The city's first electric streetcar begins operating on Church Street.

1894: The last horse-drawn streetcar retires.

1920–21: The Toronto Transportation Commission (TTC) is created by an Act of the Province. It introduces a single-fare system and

Toronto's first motorbuses.

1933: The first and still-used TTC stop poles appear; they are white with red margins at the top and bottom.

1938: The first "Red Rocket" streetcars enter service; they will eventually number 745.

1939–45: During the war, women become TTC drivers, conductors and maintenance workers for the first time.

1947: Electric trolley coaches appear.

1953: The first tokens are introduced for adult fares.

Holy Trinity

Completed in 1847 in a rundown residential area of downtown, the Anglican Church of the Holy Trinity, or "the little church beside the Eaton Centre," is now smack-dab in the middle of the city's thriving centre, close to the courts, City Hall, provincial government buildings, shopping malls and a university.

The church was built thanks to an anonymous donation with an important catch: pews were to be free—not, as was the tradition, rented or sold. This ensured a congregation drawn from the city's less affluent citizens. Over time the church ministered to downtown residents and supported social-justice causes. During the Great Depression, under the Reverend John Frank, it became known as the home of the egalitarian "social gospel," and in the 1960s and '70s the congregation began to play an important role in worship and church governance.

In the 1970s the developers of Eaton Centre planned to demolish Holy Trinity, but the church rallied support and won the right to remain. Three decades ago it opened its doors to the Metropolitan Community Church, Toronto's first church for the gay-and-lesbian community. It has regularly sponsored and supported refugees, and in 2007 the Spanish congregation of San Esteban began worshipping there. Holy Trinity's reputation for serving and advocating for the less entitled continues; it remains a tranquil oasis, dwarfed but not intimidated by the modern commercial towers surrounding it.

1954: The TTC's name changes to the Toronto Transit Commission. The city's first subway line opens on Yonge, 7.4 km between Union and Eglinton stations, and 250,000 people ride it the first day.

1961: The Metropass is introduced at a cost of $26 per month.

1963: The University subway line opens from Union Station to St. George.

1966: The Bloor-Danforth subway line opens from Keele to Woodbine.

1968: The Bloor-Danforth line extends west to Islington and east to Warden.

1973: The Yonge line is extended north to York Mills...

1974: ...and then further north to Finch.

1975: Wheel-Trans is born; it uses lift-equipped vans to transport people in wheelchairs.

1978: The Spadina subway line opens between St. George and Wilson.

1980: The Bloor-Danforth subway line extends west to Kipling and east to Kennedy.

1985: The Scarborough RT line (for rapid transit) opens between Kennedy and McCowan.

1987: The North York Centre subway station opens.

1988: TTC ridership record reports 463.5 million annual customer trips.

1996: The Spadina line extends north to Downsview.

2002: The Sheppard line opens east from Yonge to Don Mills, and the TTC's 24-billionth rider mark is reached.

2006: The first diesel-electric hybrid buses hit the streets.

They said it

"I have never [seen] anything in Europe to exceed the loathsome sights to be met within Toronto."

– William Lyon Mackenzie, Toronto's first mayor, on seeing cholera victims in 1834

They said it

"*The sleighing was never better in this part of the country than it is at present...and people...in York...are determined to enjoy it with a vengeance by driving over every foot passenger that comes their way thus verifying the old adage which says 'set a beggar on horseback, and he'll ride to the devil'.*"

– *The Canadian Freeman* newspaper, Jan. 18, 1827

COME ONE, COME ALL

From 1922 to 1955, Torontonians had their own Coney Island on the waterfront of Lake Ontario at the foot of Roncesvalles Avenue. Sunnyside Amusement Park featured popular attractions such as The Flyer rollercoaster, which boasted "the dippiest dips on the continent," the Derby Racer steeplechase ride, several merry-go-rounds, indoor and outdoor music concerts, flagpole sitting, boat burnings, fireworks displays, night clubs and restaurants. Publicly owned and offering low-cost entertainment, its wide mix of entertainment attracted both working- and middle-class Torontonians by the thousands every summer for more than three decades.

Inside the Sunnyside bathing pavilion people could change, shower and store their things using one of more than 7,700 lockers before swimming in the lake. Admission fees for the pavilion were 25 cents for an adult and 15 cents for a child, and you could rent bathing suits and towels if you didn't bring your own.

Beside the pavilion was a pool called "the Tank," which measured 91 m by 23 m and had room for up to 2,000 swimmers (adults paid 35 cents, children 10 cents). The Tank was considered the largest outdoor swimming pool in the world at the time. The boardwalk was the place to stroll and the nightclubs were the place to dance; Count Basie, Duke Ellington and Artie Shaw all played the premier venue, the Palais Royale. Sunnyside hosted an annual Easter parade, as well as the Miss Toronto pageant.

Plans to demolish the park were formed in 1943, and the demolition was finally ordered in 1955 to make room for the Gardiner Expressway project. When the fateful day arrived a few of the rides were saved, among them the Derby Racer, which was moved to the CNE grounds, and the carousel, sold to Walt Disney for Disneyland. The Palais Royale building, the pool and the bathing pavilion are the only relics of the park still in evidence today.

TAKE 5 FIVE
DEAD ZONES

1. **Garrison Cemetery:** The first military cemetery in Toronto, Victoria Square, south of Wellington, has about 400 graves, though many of the markers have been lost or destroyed. It opened in 1793, closed in 1863 and was used by those associated with Fort York. The first known body laid to rest there was Katherine Simcoe, the 15-month-old daughter of Lieutenant-Governor John Graves Simcoe and his wife, Elizabeth.

2. **St. James Cemetery:** Located at Parliament and Bloor, it opened in 1844 on the "far outside" of town boundaries and still is in use. Famous residents include the Gooderham and Worts families.

3. **Potter's Field, Yorkville:** Founded in 1826 and closed about 50 years later, it ran along Bloor Street and was used for those unqualified for religious burials. When Yorkville expanded the residents were moved to the Necropolis, then to Mount Pleasant Cemetery. It is unknown just how many unmarked graves and bodies were left behind when it was built over.

4. **Necropolis Cemetery:** Founded in 1850, it's one of Toronto's oldest and biggest, More than 40,000 people are buried here, including Toronto's first mayor, William Lyon Mackenzie, and journalist George Brown, founder of the *Globe and Mail.*

5. **Mount Pleasant Cemetery:** Founded in 1876, this huge cemetery is now one of North America's premium arboretums. Prime Minister William Lyon Mackenzie King and pianist Glenn Gould are buried there.

T.O. HEALTH BREAKTHROUGHS

- 1885: Dr. William Canniff, Toronto's first medical officer of health, urges inoculation during a smallpox outbreak, saving hundreds of lives.
- 1910: Chlorine is added to the city's drinking water, almost eliminating typhoid fever over the next 20 years and reducing deaths from 151 in 1910 to three in 1930.
- Early 1950s: A successful vaccine against polio is developed at the University of Toronto.
- 1952: Dr. Frederick Banting and Charles Best develop insulin as a treatment for diabetes.
- 1989: Doctors at the Hospital for Sick Children discover the gene responsible for causing cystic fibrosis.
- 2007: Doctors at Toronto General Hospital repair a hole in a patient's heart using a disappearing patch.
- 2009: Doctors at Mount Sinai Hospital discover a way to create stem cells from adult tissue, eliminating the need for controversial embryonic stem cells.

MARILYN BELL

In 1954 the Canadian National Exhibition, in an effort to drum up publicity, offered a $10,000 prize to world famous U.S. swimmer Florence Chadwick if she could swim across Lake Ontario. A 16-year-old Torontonian named Marilyn Bell felt the offer snubbed Canadians, so she gamely threw herself into the mix.

On Sept. 8, 1954, three swimmers set out in a bid to become the first person to swim across Lake Ontario, a distance of 51.5 km. Sustained by

Did you know. . .

that in 1899 an eight-room brick house on Bloor Street with slate roof and stone foundation went for $2,100? Today a two-bedroom unit in the Bellagio condominiums at 300 Bloor St. East rents for $1,900 a month, and a penthouse costs $2.5 million to buy.

Pablum, corn syrup and lemon juice, Bell swam for 20 hours and 59 minutes through the 21°C five-metre-high waves, with lamprey eels attacking her arms and legs. Chadwick and the other competitor, Winnie Roach, both gave up long before the finish line. When Bell reached the Toronto shore there were 300,000 people there to greet her, and the CNE awarded her the prize. Marilyn Bell was named Newsmaker of the Year by the Canadian Press, inducted into the Canada's Sports Hall of Fame in 1958 and presented with the Order of Canada in 2002.

From Whisky to Culture

Toronto's waterfront, once the site of intense industrial activity, is slowly being transformed into more intriguing people spaces. One of the most distinctive of those areas is the Distillery District, near the mouth of the Don River. The unique history and architecture of this site at 55 Mill St. is preserved today largely because it remained a working factory for liquor giant Gooderham & Worts from the mid-1800s until 1990.

British immigrant James Worts first built a gristmill on the site in 1831, powered by a 21-metre-tall windmill that became an easily identifiable marker for sailors over the next quarter century. The location allowed easy access to shipping by boat and, later, by rail. William Gooderham, Worts' brother-in-law, arrived a year later with 54 family members and soon had to assume control of the business. (Worts committed suicide in the company well in 1834 following his wife's death in childbirth.)

A surplus of wheat in 1837 led Gooderham and James Worts Jr. to try making whisky and beer. At the time Toronto had a tavern for every 100 people, and beer was the equivalent of water. The population was surging, fuelled by an influx of Irish immigrants. They in turn fed the distillery's success by increasing local demand and supplied the company with a new pool of labourers. By the 1870s the Gooderham and Worts Distillery was shipping more than a million gallons of spirits across Canada and into the United States and South America. It was

FOOD AND DRINK

Food in early Toronto was either fresh, because surrounding farms were plentiful, or preserved by salting or smoking. British traditions dominated. Joseph Willcocks, writing in his diary in the fall of 1800, reported eating ham, chicken, tongue, stewed beef, minced veal, bread pudding, mutton, turnip, wild duck and peach pie. Today almost every known ethnic cuisine is available in Toronto, either in restaurants or for home preparation, in all price ranges.

Alcohol appeared early in the city. In 1810 locally brewed whiskey cost

the province's largest liquor producer, turning out nearly half of all spirits made in Ontario by 1871.

The architectural legacy of the distillery's success is not confined to the factory site. William Gooderham built Little Trinity Church, and the company erected worker-cottages around Trinity and Sackville. In 1891 George Gooderham, who took over the business from his father, William, built the Gooderham "Flatiron" Building at Wellington and Front, which remains one of downtown Toronto's most distinctive landmarks. In 1889 he built a mansion at the corner of Bloor and St. George, which is now used as the York Club.

Business boomed along until World War I, when the distillery developed a sideline: manufacturing acetone. Then Prohibition created business setbacks. In 1926 Gooderham and Worts merged with the Hiram Walker Company, and the distillery marshalled on. G&W whisky, rum and antifreeze were produced on-site until 1990.

Today more than 40 brick-and-stone industrial buildings remain, unified by design and all built between 1859 and 1927. After a couple of unsuccessful attempts at conversion, the property was bought in 2001 by Cityscape Development Corp. and extensively refurbished by Wallace Studios. It reopened in 2003 as a pedestrian-only complex dedicated to arts, culture and entertainment. Covering 5.3 hectares, the Distillery District is the largest and best-preserved collection of Victorian industrial architecture in North America and Toronto's only heritage district.

They said it

25 cents to 50 cents a gallon, and many found the money to partake. The first temperance societies began to appear in the 1830s, a response to the plethora of drinking establishments and a population keen on imbibing. The movement took hold during the following decades, despite a parallel phenomenal growth in distilling in the city. Ontario passed its prohibition laws in 1916, and they stayed on the books until 1927. West Toronto voted to become dry in 1904 and didn't become wet again until 1999.

Did you know...

that City of Toronto officials reputedly said that the one good thing that came out of the great cholera outbreaks of 1932–34 was that the threat of a fatal disease stopped residents from dumping their outhouse pails onto the street?

Did you know...

that in 1907 the city deemed tobogganing in its parks on Sundays illegal?

They said it

"You build your stations like we build our cathedrals."
– HRH The Prince of Wales, at the opening of Union Station, 1927

Weblinks

HisTORicity: Toronto Then and Now

historicity.torontopubliclibrary.ca

The Toronto Public Library, founded in 1883, is working to digitize its archival records in order to increase the public's access to historic and often fragile documents. This site contains maps, city directories and pictures of Toronto, both historical and current.

Toronto Star: Looking Back

www.thestar.com/news/torontogta/localhistory

This site contains fairly recent stories from the Toronto Star about old events and happenings. It includes reflections about the events, buildings and people that have made Toronto the city it is today.

City of Toronto Archives

www.toronto.ca/archives

Some material from the archives is available online, including information about a range of aspects of Toronto's history. The website also allows you to search for information that is available at the Archives' massive facility on Spadina Road. There are instructions for tracing the history of your house, and you can copy old pictures and articles for a small fee.

Did you know. . .

that the first apartment building in Toronto wasn't constructed until 1903? There were four by 1905 and 113 by 1913.

Crime and Punishment

CRIMELINE

1798: York's first jail opens on King Street East, where the King Edward Hotel is now located. On Oct. 11, John Sullivan is the first prisoner executed in town; he was convicted of stealing a forged note with a value of about a dollar.

1815: The first keeper at the Gibraltar Point lighthouse, John Paul Radelmuller, is murdered. Two men are arrested but not convicted. Some say Radelmuller's ghost still haunts the lighthouse.

1819: A farmhand named DeBenyon is lynched near the Don River by an enraged mob after the brutal murder of his stepson.

1830: York, with a population of approximately 6,000, has about 60 taverns and just as many brothels.

1834: The Toronto City Police Service is established. Its only full-time constable relies on a band of volunteers to help enforce the law in the 9,000-person city. Toronto Mayor William Lyon Mackenzie orders a convict confined to public stocks as part of his sentence for petty larceny.

1838: Ten thousand people gather by the jail at King and Toronto streets to watch the execution of Samuel Lount and Peter Matthews, two participants in Mackenzie's failed Upper Canada Rebellion.

1840s: Toronto's mayor, William Henry Boulton, is charged with running a brothel. He steps down from office briefly and is exonerated by the courts; his tenant, who kept a tavern on the premises in question, loses his licence.

1840s and '50s: The most common offence committed in Toronto is larceny, including cattle theft.

1852 to 1858: Six major riots take place between rival Irish factions, the Protestants versus the Catholics, in the city.

1870s: Toronto has roughly one bar for every 150 residents. The bars sell Caribbean rum and locally brewed whisky for high profit. Imbibing leads to disorderly conduct, and city jailhouses fill with people charged with excessive drinking.

Corporal Punishment in Old Toronto

One of the most brutal aspects of life in York was the system of corporal punishment. For example, British colonial authorities were fond of branding prisoners on the tongue or hand. Until 1798, convicted felons received their punishment in public on Berkeley Street, today's Front Street.

Branding was abolished in 1802, except in cases of manslaughter, but authorities still had plenty of other grim ways to punish wrongdoers. Whipping was common for petty larceny (theft under $10) and was administered in public until 1830, near where the St. Lawrence Market stands today. Prisoners were typically given 39 lashes from the cat-o'-nine-tails.

They said it

"Houses of ill-fame in Toronto? Certainly not. The whole city is an immense house of ill fame, the roof of which is the blue canopy of heaven during the summer months."

– C.S. Clark, *Of Toronto the Good* (1898)

1883: Toronto police acquire a horse-drawn van and no longer have to walk suspects back to the station.

1880: George Brown, a Father of Confederation and founder of the *Globe*, which will become the *Globe and Mail*, is shot in the leg by one of the paper's disgruntled employees; he dies when the wound becomes infected.

1892: John Radclive is appointed Canada's first professional hangman. He buys a nice house in Toronto's west end with his new federal salary.

1894: Toronto's police service becomes the first in North America to use bicycles. The following year the members acquire their first boat to combat illegal fishing, shooting and bathing.

1895: Clara Ford, a mixed-race seamstress known to dress in men's clothing, is tried for the murder of Frank Westwood, a well-to-do young Parkdale man shot when he answered his door late at night. Ford admitted guilt to the police, then retracted her confession on the stand and was found not guilty by the jury. At one point during the investigation, Arthur Conan Doyle is invited to help solve the murder.

1901: Constable William Boyd is the first Toronto policeman killed in the line of duty.

1904: A Toronto West End neighbourhood goes dry to end drunken rowdiness. Residents of West Toronto, now called The Junction, ban alcohol to stop fights between men working in the railway stockyards. A series of failed referendums leaves The Junction dry until 1997.

TAKE 5 JAMES DUBRO'S FIVE
INFAMOUS TORONTO ORGANIZED-CRIME HITS

James Dubro is a past president of Crime Writers of Canada, the winner of its 2002 Derrick Murdoch Award and the author of five best-selling books on organized crime in Canada, notably *Mob Rule: Inside the Canadian Mafia* and *Dragons of Crime: Asian Mobs in Canada*. His crime expertise is sought for television, magazine and other projects. Dubro has lived in Toronto since 1970.

1. **High Noon in Chinatown: A Jagged Bottle Across the Throat:** Richard Castro was the treasurer of the Kung Lok Triad, an Asian organized-crime gang founded in the mid-1970s that ran extortion, gambling and other underworld activities in Toronto's Chinatown. On July 12, 1981, he was lunching at the elegant China Court Restaurant on Spadina Avenue. Four men, some of whom owed money to the Kung Lok for gambling debts, followed him out of the restaurant, then two of them slashed his jugular vein with a broken beer bottle. The Kung Lok was put on notice that they were no longer the supreme leaders of organized crime in Chinatown.

2. **Mafioso "Paulie the Fox" is Cornered:** The longest-running and best known Mafia boss in Toronto was Paul Volpe. Known as Paulie by friends and "the Fox" by rivals, Volpe ran the largest mob family in the city from the 1950s to 1983. He began his criminal life as a bootlegger in the 1940s and became a major criminal force in loan-sharking, gambling, construction unions, extortion and other major mob activities. On Nov. 14, 1983, his bullet-ridden remains were found in the trunk of his wife's BMW at Toronto's Pearson International Airport. The assassination is still unsolved; suspects range from rival Mafioso in Toronto, Hamilton, and Montreal to mobsters based in Atlantic City, where Volpe had been involved in real estate.

3. **Gang Boss Mowed Down on Dundas:** Vietnamese gang boss Asau Tran, who came to Canada in 1979 from refugee camps in Hong Kong, was one of the most ruthless bosses of Toronto's Chinatown until his life ended on Aug. 16, 1991. That's when two well-dressed

men gunned down Tran, his 27-year-old girlfriend and a third man at 3 a.m. outside a Chinese restaurant on Dundas Street. The brazen murders were never solved, though police suspect the hit was organized by a rival Vietnamese gang leader. The summer of 1991 saw more than 10 murders in and around Chinese and Vietnamese restaurants in Toronto, as Vietnamese gangs fought for territory.

4. **Boxer "Hurricane" Melo Goes Down for the Count:** Portuguese national Eddie Melo was a colourful figure in the boxing world and the Toronto underworld from the late 1970s until his murder in 2001. A middleweight boxer with 27 knockouts to his credit, "Hurricane" Melo was also an enforcer and extortionist for the mob in Toronto and a long-time close associate of the late Montreal mob boss Frank Cotroni. On April 6, 2001, at about 6:30 p.m., Melo was sitting in his wife's Jeep Cherokee with his associate Joao "Johnny" Pavao at Mississauga's Cliffway Plaza. Suddenly, a man appeared and shot and killed both men, blasting Melo twice in the head. In 2003 Charles Gagne, a 33-year-old Montreal-based hit man, pleaded guilty to the contract hit, but no one has been convicted of paying him his $75,000 fee. Ironically, at the time of his murder Melo had been fighting deportation to Portugal, where he might have been much safer.

5. **A Most "Unprofessional" Hit—A Settling of Mob Accounts Goes Very Wrong:** On April 21, 2004, Louise Russo was almost killed inside a California Sandwich shop in North Toronto in a spray of bullets let loose by hit men working for Mafioso Pietro "Peter" Scarcella. The actual target—Michael Modica, an Italian Mafioso—was unscathed. The 45-year-old Russo, who had just left a Toronto Catholic school board meeting, was buying a treat for his daughter. She barely survived; her spine was severed and she is now confined to a wheelchair. In a 2006 plea bargain, Scarcella got 11 years for the botched hit and agreed to the Crown's proposal to pay Russo $2 million in compensation. Two other people, including Paris Christoforou, a Hells Angels member, were also convicted.

1905: The Don Jail moves its executions indoors from the prison courtyard.

1913: The first Toronto policewomen are hired and allowed to make patrols. They will not be issued guns until the 1970s.

1917: Police cars are introduced for detectives.

Settling Scores in Old York

For a short while in the early 1800s, York imported the "gentlemanly" European tradition of addressing wrongs by aiming pistols at close range. The first recorded duel in town was instigated at the highest level of society. In January of 1800, Major John Small, clerk of the Executive Council, shot and killed John White, Canada's first attorney general. The path to the gunfight hinged on women's honour and a "he said/she said" gossip trail.

Apparently, Mrs. Small and a friend had discussed their disapproval of Mrs. White. When he heard of their behaviour, Mr. White made disparaging remarks about Mrs. Small to a friend. Several months later, word of his remarks got back to the Smalls, at which point the offended husband challenged Mr. White to a duel. Both men met the next morning with their seconds; they fired at the same instant, and Mr. White was felled. Mr. Small was acquitted of murder at his trial, as was the custom for duellists.

York's second duel was slated for July of 1801 between a Mr. Weeks and a Mr. Willcocks but was prevented by the arrest of Mr. Willcocks en route to the location. Another did not take place until April of 1812, when Colonel MacDonnell and Dr. Warren Baldwin crossed to Gibraltar Point to fight. This one ended bloodlessly: at the moment of truth, the Colonel declined to fire at his friend and Baldwin shot his pistol into the air. The two men apparently remained the best of friends.

1933: A huge riot at Christie Pits, a Toronto park, erupts between a Jewish softball team and their swastika-brandishing Anglo-Canadian opponents.

1952: The Boyd Gang escapes from the Don Jail for a second time and triggers a huge manhunt.

1957: Thirteen separate police services across the Toronto area are amalgamated into the Metropolitan Toronto Police Force.

1962: Canada's last public execution occurs at the Don Jail, a double hanging of Arthur Lucas, who killed an undercover narcotics agent, and Ronald Turpin, who killed a police officer when fleeing a robbery.

Brooks' Bush Gang Strikes Again

On March 30, 1861, four duck hunters rowing on Toronto's Don River discovered a body floating in the shallow water. Although it was badly decomposed, it was determined to be that of John Sheridan Hogan—an Irish immigrant, lawyer, Parliament member and prize-winning writer—who had disappeared on Dec. 1, 1859.

A police informer reported that Hogan had been robbed and murdered by James Brown, Jane Ward, John Sherrick and two other members of the Brooks' Bush Gang. Apparently, on the night of Hogan's disappearance, he had left a friend's house and walked east on Kingston Road. At the Don Bridge he showed a large sum of money, then was beaten and killed after offering to pay a large "toll" to the gang members to get across.

In one of Toronto's most gripping murder cases, several people were charged and tried but only one, James Brown, was convicted. Brown's execution on March 10, 1862, was the city's last public hanging.

1968: Toronto police acquire their first in-house computer; it's used for storing crime statistics.

1972: Two police officers, Det. Michael Irwin and Det. Douglas Sinclair, are gunned down when called to a residence where a tenant with a lengthy criminal record is being evicted.

1977: Rolling Stones guitarist Keith Richards is arrested in Toronto's Harbour Castle Hotel after police find 22 grams of heroin and five grams of cocaine in his possession.

1981: Police raid several bath houses downtown that cater to a homosexual clientele, arresting more than 300 men. It is the second largest mass arrest in Canada, surpassed only by arrests during the 1970 FLQ crisis. The raids spark fierce protests and galvanize the city's gay community.

The Curious Case of Clara Ford

After returning home from a night out with friends on Saturday, Oct. 6, 1894, Frank Westwood, the eighteen-year-old son of a well-off white family, answered the front door of his father's house in Toronto's Parkdale neighbourhood. Westwood, who was shot once, described the culprit as a mid-sized man he didn't recognize wearing a dark suit and fedora.

Before Westwood died four days later, the Toronto police questioned him at length. Several well-attended inquests were held over the next five weeks. In time, it became evident that the gunman had been a woman dressed in man's clothes.

On Nov. 20 Clara Ford, a 33-year-old "mulatto" seamstress who had once lived next to the Westwoods, was charged. Initially denying involvement, she later confessed, claiming she shot Westwood because he had previously assaulted her. On the fourth day of the trial in May of 1895, Ford retracted her confession, insisting the police had tricked her into making it. The jury of twelve men found her not guilty.

Toronto's Gentleman Bandit

Edwin Alonzo Boyd was a handsome, charismatic and an incorrigible thief whose bank-robbing sprees terrorized and titillated Torontonians in the 1950s. The son of a Toronto police officer, Boyd left home when his mother died and drifted aimlessly across Canada during the Depression, committing petty crimes along the way. A spell in the army briefly straightened him out, and by the late 1940s he was married and driving a Toronto streetcar. On Sept. 9, 1949, he abruptly switched career paths, holding up a Bank of Montreal for $2,000.

Boyd kept on robbing until late 1951, when he was caught and sent to the Don Jail. There, two violent convicts, Lennie Jackson, a former hairdresser from Niagara Falls, and Willie "The Clown" Jackson (no relation), convinced Boyd to join their escape plan. The three men broke out and soon caught up with another criminal, Steve Suchan, a former violinist who had traded his violin for a couple of guns. When that foursome started robbing banks, tales of "The Boyd Gang" started appearing in the papers. The flamboyant Boyd liked to jump on bank counters, guns in hand, and announce that a robbery was in progress. The public was shocked, although the press portrayed Boyd as a non-violent "gentleman bandit."

In December of 1951, Willie Jackson was arrested in Montreal. Three months later, Lennie Jackson and Suchan shot and killed a Toronto police officer who had stopped their vehicle. Jackson and Suchan were captured, then Boyd. All four robbers were placed in the same section of the Don Jail, and the reunited Boyd Gang promptly escaped again.

This time a dragnet of 2,000 policemen was deployed. They found and captured the quartet in a local barn. On Dec. 16, 1952, Lennie Jackson and Suchan were hanged for murder. Boyd was paroled in the mid-1960s and moved to British Columbia, living what for him was a low-key life; he died in 2002 at age 88. Not long after, CBC-TV aired a documentary that suggested he had committed offences for which he was never caught, including murder. If that's true, it puts the lie to the Boyd's reputation as the "gentleman bandit."

Mid-1980s: The "balcony rapist" terrorizes women in the Church and Wellesley area of Toronto. One victim takes the police to court for failing to alert women about the threat in their area.

1994: Georgina (Vivi) Leimonis is shot by three heavily armed Jamaican-born gangsters in a bungled robbery at Just Desserts, an upscale Toronto café; she dies the next day. The shooting raises questions about race relations and public safety.

2002: Toronto Mayor Mel Lastman is photographed shaking hands with a member of the Hells Angels biker gang, which was then engaged in a violent war with a rival gang in Quebec. Lastman pleads ignorance about the Hells Angels' criminal activities.

2002: Constable Laura Ellis, killed in a vehicle accident, is the first female policewoman to die in the line of duty.

2005: Jane Creba, a 15-year-old innocent bystander, is killed on Boxing Day after two alleged gangs start shooting at each other on Yonge Street. Creba's pointless death awakens the city to the threat of gang violence.

2006: Police arrest more than 100 suspects associated with a gang called the Jamestown Crew in the largest anti-gang crackdown in Toronto history. They also arrest members of an alleged Islamic terrorist cell in the GTA.

Did you know. . .

that in the 1830s, any York tavern that had an "Oysters and hot coffee always ready" sign hanging over the door was advertising that a prostitute was on shift?

2007: Fifteen year-old Jordan Manners is shot and killed at C.W. Jefferys Collegiate Institute in North York; a police lockdown ensues. Two teenagers are charged, and the murder sets off a huge debate about gun control and school safety. In December, Aqsa Parvez dies in what is dubbed the city's first "honour killing."

Sex, Lies and Videotape

Sexual sadist Paul Bernardo and his accomplice wife, Karla Homolka, committed most of their crimes in St. Catharines, Ont., but Toronto was hauled into the lurid spotlight when Bernardo's trial was held there in the summer of 1995. The case became a media circus, with an enormous crush of reporters and members of the public clamouring to get into the courtroom.

Bernardo kidnapped, raped and killed two teenage girls, Leslie Mahaffy and Kristen French, and indirectly caused the death of a third: Karla's younger sister, Tammy. Bernardo committed several sexual assaults in Scarborough in the late 1980s and is suspected of killing additional women. His trial featured huge line-ups outside the courthouse and a bizarre display of videotaped evidence. The accused was an obsessive videographer, recording criminal sex-torture sessions as well as sexual romps with his wife. In court, the criminal tapes were subject to strict controls; the audio was broadcast for all to hear but only the jury could see the footage.

On Sept. 1, 1995, Bernardo was found guilty of murder and a slate of sexual offences. A decade later, Karla—with whom Crown attorneys had cut a deal in exchange for testimony against her husband—was released from prison. Bernardo himself will likely be incarcerated for the rest of his life. His trial remains one of Toronto's most disturbing court cases.

2008: In September, Toronto police start patrols in about two dozen Catholic and public schools, hoping to prevent further violence. In November, C.W. Jefferys Collegiate is back in the spotlight when a 16-year-old male student is stabbed, but not killed, in the building. C.W. Jefferys is not one of the schools patrolled by police.

Lord of Crossharbour

Canada's trial of this century surprisingly didn't happen in Canada, nor did it involve a Canadian citizen. In 2007, however, every newspaper and media outlet across the country had their most seasoned staffers at the Conrad Black trial in Chicago. For better or worse, Black had been part of the Canadian conversation for almost 40 years.

With the publication of the Peter C. Newman book *The Canadian Establishment* in 1975 and a subsequent television series, Black emerged as the ultimate Establishment star. Young, patrician and erudite, he embraced privilege and the execution of power as if it were handed down by divine right.

Although Black's business empire can be said to have begun with his first newspaper purchase in 1966, in 1976 he pulled off perhaps his biggest and most important coup, mercilessly seizing control of the Argus Corporation after the death of John Angus "Bud" McDougald. The coup gave Black, a small newspaper-chain owner, major interests in Labrador Mining, Noranda Mines, Hollinger-Argus, Standard Broadcasting, Dominion Stores, Domtar and Massey-Ferguson.

The steady growth of the Black holdings surprised no one, as the man had played hardball all his life. Companies were jettisoned, and he fought incursions into his power with all the legal might available to him. He removed a $56 million surplus from the Dominion Stores

2009: Inspector Kathryn Martin, a 24-year veteran of the Toronto Police Service, is appointed the new head of its homicide squad, the fifth largest in North America. She is the first woman named to the position, one of the most sought-after in the organization.

workers' pension plan, for which John Ralston Saul described him as a "stripper of assets" rather than a capitalist.

Black's real interests, though, were in newspapers and magazines. They were at once enormously profitable and an instrument from which he could, and did, provide the masses with his views on everything from health care and democracy to the United States and capitalism. Perhaps no sweeter moment came for Black as the morning on which he launched the *National Post* daily newspaper.

When Britain came calling in 2001 with the offer of a Lordship, Black assumed his title as if it were not a surprise but an expectation. But neither his knowledge of British history and his long-held admiration for capitalist Britain and the U.S., nor his retinue of rich and powerful friends, could protect him from the arm of American prosecution.

In the period leading up to his trial for racketeering, obstruction of justice, money laundering and wire fraud, Black returned to Toronto and cautiously re-entered the social circuit as if he were looking for familiar and predictable terrain. Today, of course, the man who was once the embodiment of the Canadian Establishment sits in a Florida jail, widely reviled and an object of Canadians' gleeful disdain, including a few whose sinecure flowed from Black's erstwhile largesse.

CRIME IN TORONTO

In 2007 Toronto had the lowest rate of criminal code offences, excluding traffic, of any Canadian city with more 500,000 people. Toronto's crime rate (4,461 offences per 100,000 people) was lower than Winnipeg's (9,644 offences per 100,000), Edmonton's (9,572), Vancouver's (9,136), Calgary's (6,202), Montreal's (5,958), Hamilton's (5,511), Ottawa's (5,457) and Quebec City's (4,524), all of which are smaller cities. South of the border, New York City rang in at 2,517 criminal offences per 100,000 people, Los Angeles at 3,505 and Houston 7,006.

TAKE 5 FIVE TORONTO
COLD CASES

1. **Donna Stearne and Wendy Tedford:** On April 27, 1973, a teenage boy on his way to school discovered the bodies of 17-year-old high school students Stearne and Tedford in a vacant lot. The two close friends had gone shopping at Yorkdale Mall the night before and had stopped at a restaurant to have soft drinks; both girls were shot in the head shortly after leaving. Ballistic tests indicated the murder weapon was a .38-calibre revolver stolen from a Windsor, Ont., home.

2. **Alexander Romeo LeBlanc:** A member of Toronto's fledgling openly gay community, which was just coming out of the closet in the late 1970s, LeBlanc lived downtown and managed a dance club. On Sept. 20, 1978, his friends became concerned when they couldn't contact him. They went to his apartment, forced their way inside and found his body; he had been stabbed repeatedly. There are no known suspects.

3. **Christine Prince:** A Welsh nanny living in Canada, Prince and a female friend went to a movie at Yonge and Bloor on June 20, 1982. Afterward they met Prince's boyfriend, walked to a doughnut shop and, at around 1:20 a.m., headed for the subway. Prince and her girlfriend boarded a westbound streetcar at the St. Clair West station

In 2007 there was also a five percent decrease in overall reported crime in Toronto. Murders did increase by 20 percent over 2006 (from 70 to 84), but sexual assaults decreased 3.8 percent and total robberies dropped by 3.6 percent. Toronto's homicide rate in 2007 (2 per 100,000) was lower than Winnipeg's (3.6 per 100,000), Edmonton's (3.3), Vancouver's (2.4) and Calgary's (3.1). It was higher than Montreal's, Hamilton's and Ottawa's (all of which stood at 1.6 per 100,000). New York City had a homicide rate of 7.3 per 100,000 people, Los Angeles 12.4, and Houston 18.2.

Sources: Statistics Canada, City of Toronto, U.S. Department of Justice

and the friend got off first. Prince was supposed to get off a couple stops later and walk home, but she never made it; her nude body was found in the West Rouge River two days later. She had drowned, and bruises and abrasions on her head, face and body indicated that she had been beaten.

4. **Susan Tice and Erin Harrison Gilmour:** A 45-year-old mother of four, Tice had separated from her husband and moved from Calgary to live alone in Toronto. Gilmour was a 22-year-old who lived on Hazelton Avenue. Tice was found dead from multiple stab wounds on Aug. 17, 1983; Gilmour on the following Dec. 20. The two women didn't know each other, but DNA evidence indicated that they were likely killed by the same man.

5. **Simone Sandler:** A personable young woman who worked as a film recruiter, Sandler's job was to stand next to a sandwich board that read "Extras for films" and record the names of those who expressed interest. She was last seen working on July 23, 1994; her parents contacted police when she failed to return home. A week later, her partially clothed body was recovered from the Don River; she had been strangled.

They said it

"Who in blazes was such a fool to put them in one cell block? The men were allowed to eat together, sleep together and were practically given club car privileges...it's pretty shabby treatment for our police who have done all they can and are let down like this."
  – Toronto Mayor Allan Lamport, Sept. 8, 1952, upon learning that The Boyd Gang had escaped from prison a second time

CRIME BY THE NUMBERS (2007)

- Criminal-code offences: 194,151
- Homicides: 84
- Assaults: 24,669
- Robberies: 5,695
- Break and enters: 14,272
- Sexual assaults: 2,455
- Persons charged with drug violations: 6,656
- Persons charged with drinking-and-driving offences: 2,107
- Persons charged with violent crimes: 14,873
- Stolen vehicles: 8,447

Source: City of Toronto

They said it

"Then there was the rumour that a certain Toronto bank was protected by machine guns. Just how the machine guns were to be cut loose on the robbers was never explained. The origins of this rumour are the two German Maxims—war souvenirs—which flank the entrance to the vault of the Canadian Bank of Commerce."
  – Ernest Hemingway, writing in the *Toronto Star*, Dec. 1, 1923

POLICING TORONTO BY THE NUMBERS (2007)

- Number of police officers employed in Toronto: 5,558
- Number of police officers employed in Canada: 64,000
- Ratio of police officers to Toronto citizens: 1:495
- Number of men employed: 4,642
- Number of women employed: 916
- Number of police stations: 17
- Number of police vehicles: 1,561
- Number of police boats: 23
- Number of police horses: 28
- Total calls to police communications centre: 1,790,045
- Emergency calls: 928,955
- Non-emergency calls: 861,090
- Calls to police in Chinese: 1,999
- Calls to police in Spanish: 576
- Calls to police in Italian: 227

Source: Toronto Police Service, Statistics Canada

TORONTO POLICE SERVICE BASE SALARIES (2009)

Cadet in training	$45,042.34
4th-class constable	$50,057.71
3rd-class constable	$57,211.20
2nd-class constable	$64,364.69
1st-class constable	$71,522.91

Source: Toronto Police Service

Did you know. . .

that in the 1860s, Toronto police constables had to have permission from the police chief to marry, and the newlyweds had to live in a "respectable" part of Toronto? Single constables were housed in special police barracks.

STOLEN CARS

Toronto has a motor-vehicle theft rate of 279 per 100,000 people, considerably lower than Winnipeg's (1,714 per 100,000), Edmonton's (832), Vancouver's (630), Calgary's (639), Montreal's (601) and Hamilton's (481). It is just higher than Ottawa's (264 per 100,000) and Quebec City's (216).

Source: Statistics Canada

IMPAIRED DRIVING

Toronto police charged 2,107 people with drinking-and-driving offences in 2007. In Canada, there were a total of 79,513 impaired driving incidents the same year. The highest rate in the country was in the Northwest Territories (1,801 incidents per 100,000 people). At 139 incidents per 100,000 people, Ontario has the lowest rate of impaired-driving charges in Canada.

Source: Statistic Canada, Toronto Police Service

FINE, THEN

- Car parked more than 30 cm from curb: $15
- Car obstructing a driveway/laneway: $40
- Car stopped on a bridge: $60
- Car parked within 3 m of a fire hydrant: $100
- Car parked illegally in a fire route: $250

Did you know. . .

that when not performing his official duties, Canada's first professional hangman, John Radclive, sometimes worked as a steward at Toronto's Sunnyside Boating Club? A heavy drinker, in 1911 Radclive died in his Fern Avenue home of cirrhosis of the liver.

- Car parked in a disabled-parking location: $450
- Failure to remove snow and ice from your sidewalk: $105
- Failure to licence your dog or cat: $240
- Smoking in enclosed workplaces and public places: $5,000 maximum per person

Source: City of Toronto

TRAFFIC COLLISIONS (2007)
- Total traffic collisions: 56,026
- Number of injury collisions: 11,632
- Number of people injured: 16,519
- Number of fatal collisions: 57
- Number of people killed: 57
- Number of collisions that resulted in property damage: 44,394

Source: Toronto Police Service

YOUTH CRIME
Violent crimes are homicide and homicide-related offences, sexual assaults, sexual offences, non-sexual assaults, abductions and robberies. In Toronto in 2007, some 2,770 young offenders aged 12 to 17 were charged with such crimes, comprising 15.9 percent of all such arrests in the city. Fifteen of the charges were for murder. Nationally that same year, about 176,000 youth were accused of committing a criminal offence, down two percent from 2006; of them, 74 were accused of murder, down from 85 in 2006.

Youth only led Toronto's crime stats in one category; they were charged with almost half the robberies: 1,099, or 47.7 percent of the total. The 25-to-34 age group committed the most break and enters (25.6 percent of total), non-sexual assaults (24.7 percent), sexual assaults (24.3 percent) and drinking-and-driving offences (30.4 percent). The 18-to-24 age group led in violations of the Controlled Drugs and Substances Act (32.7 percent).

Source: City of Toronto, Statistics Canada

CORRECTIONAL FACILITIES

There are four correctional centres in the GTA. Typically they house offenders serving between 60 days to two years less a day:

- Mimico Correctional Centre, 457 beds, Toronto
- Ontario Correctional Institute, 228 beds, Brampton
- Vanier Centre for Women, 124 beds, Milton
- Maplehurst Correctional Complex, 1,550 beds, Milton

Jails are older institutions established by counties or municipalities. Typically they and correctional centres house prisoners who are on remand, serving short terms or awaiting transportation to a federal or provincial facility. Toronto has just one: the 561-bed Toronto Jail (aka the Don Jail).

Detention centres are larger, more modern facilities that serve several regions. There are two in Toronto and a third in the works:

- Toronto East Detention Centre, 473 beds, Scarborough
- Toronto West Detention Centre, 631 beds, Rexdale

Additional facilities are on the way. A new secure-custody institution for 192 young offenders, the Roy McMurtry Youth Centre, was scheduled to open in Brampton in 2009. And the province has plans for a new 1,650-bed facility, the Toronto South Detention Centre, in Mimico. The Toronto Intermittent Centre, a minimum-security facility for prisoners serving weekend sentences, will also be built on the site.

Did you know. . .

that James Earl Ray hid out in Toronto after assassinating American civil rights leader Martin Luther King in Memphis, Tennessee, in April of 1968? In May, the shooter flew from Toronto to London and was arrested at Heathrow Airport.

CRIME STOPPERS

Toronto got its first Crime Stoppers program in 1984. Using TV re-enactments and other means, the organization spotlights specific crimes and encourages citizens to phone in leads. In 2007 Toronto Crime Stoppers received 7,555 tips, which led to 518 arrests, 797 cases cleared and 1,959 charges laid—and the seizure of $9,997,673 worth of property and $60,853,605 worth of drugs. Since its inception, 50,247 tips have been phoned or mailed to Toronto Crime Stoppers. The results? Almost 9,000 arrests, 13,707 cases cleared, 29,017 charges laid and $36,876,377 worth of property and $194,149,264 worth of drugs seized.

Source: Crime Stoppers

NEVER MET A BIKE HE DIDN'T LIKE

Eccentric bike-shop owner Igor Kenk was well-known to Toronto cyclists, but not just because he ran The Bicycle Clinic on Queen Street West. For years rumours had circulated that he also specialized in reselling stolen bicycles. In July of 2008, Toronto police arrested Kenk following a sting operation. A search of his home, store and rented garages turned up an astonishing 3,000 bikes, most apparently stolen, not to mention a supply of illegal drugs.

Did you know...

that when Toronto policewomen finally got permission to pack heat in the 1970s, they were given specially designed handbags, not holsters, to carry their service revolvers?

Did you know...

that Canada's first Drug Court was launched in Toronto in 1998 to give low-level, non-violent drug offenders an opportunity to receive treatment instead of jail time? Canada's first Mental Health Court opened in T.O. that same year.

Politics

Early civic government in York consisted largely of patronage appointments designed to look after British interests. In 1834, when the town became the City of Toronto and the colony's first incorporated municipality, it gained all the political machinery and institutions that properly belonged to its new status. In the first elections, men voted for controllers and aldermen in five wards but the mayor was selected by council.

Nineteenth-century civic politics were mostly conservative in nature, backed quietly by the Family Compact and the Orange Order. As the city continued to grow, mayors were faced with increasing demands for urban services. Early mayors were cautious and stand out as being products of their times. Mayor Tommy Church managed the city through World War I, and Mayor Nathan Phillips ushered in an era of unforeseen prosperity.

In April of 1953, the Ontario legislature created the Municipality of Metropolitan Toronto, the country's first metropolitan government. The existing 13 jurisdictions—Etobicoke, North York, Scarborough and York, plus the small urban communities of East York, Forest Hill, Leaside, Long Branch, Mimico, New Toronto, Swansea, Weston and the City of Toronto—were reorganized as Metro Toronto. Over time, the Metro chairman, elected by the individual councils, came to replace the Toronto mayor as the major player in civic politics.

In 1998 the provincial government once again inserted itself into the city's set-up. Despite much opposition, it did away with the existing metropolitan structure and amalgamated its former member municipalities into one huge megacity. This effectively merged the former Regional municipality of Metropolitan Toronto with the former suburb cities of Scarborough, East York, York, North York and Etobicoke.

The new civic structure now consists of a mayor and 44 councillors who represent wards across the city. Toronto city council is now the main governing and legislative body, and the mayor is the only member of council who is elected by voters. The mayor has one vote on council and is a voting member, by right of his office, at all standing committees of council.

CITY GOVERNMENT TODAY

Each of Toronto's city councillors represents between 55,000 and 65,000 people, about the same total number of people that MPs from Nunavut, Yukon, Manitoba and Alberta combined represent in the House of Commons.

Party politics are not an overt part of the municipal system at Toronto City Hall, but throughout council's history both councillors and the mayor have had direct connections or identifiable leanings. After World War II, the many challenges facing the city, including a severe housing shortage, led to some radicalism, reflected in the elec-

Did you know. . .

that the first black politician elected in Toronto civic politics was William Peyton Hubbard (1842–1935), who was elected alderman in 1894? Hubbard served on council for 15 years in several posts. Born in Toronto, he was the son of a freed slave from Virginia.

tion of Communist Party members to all levels of government throughout the 1940s and 1950s. Both right and left continue to be represented on council, and allegiances often form along party lines.

The city's governing structure was reinforced on Jan. 1, 2007, when the province passed *The City of Toronto Act* (2006), also known as Bill 53. The legislation created a "constitution" for Toronto that gave its council new powers, including the ability to create taxes, the authority to enter into agreements with the federal government, greater control over bylaws and land-planning decisions and the ability of committees to make some decisions without having to go back to council for approval. Alberta, British Columbia, Manitoba and Saskatchewan have also introduced similar legislation for some or all of their municipalities.

Bill 53 also created a new executive branch of council: the chair of each of the city's seven Standing Policy Committees plus the mayor, deputy mayor and four councillors-at-large appointed by council. While not quite achieving the "strong mayor" status of many American cities, Toronto's mayor now has more control over council than ever before.

MAYOR PRIMER

- First mayor: William Lyon Mackenzie
- Number of mayors who have served since 1900: 34
- Youngest mayor: John Powell, the city's fifth mayor, who was 29 when appointed to the position in 1838.
- Oldest mayor: Thomas Foster, who was 73 when elected in 1925.
- Longest-serving mayor: Depends on the criteria used. Art Eggleton was mayor of the old Toronto for nine years, but Mel Lastman served 25 years as mayor of North York, followed by six years as the first post-amalgamation mayor.
- Shortest-serving mayor: David Breckenridge Read served less than two months, from Nov. 11 to Dec. 31, 1858, after being appointed by council to finish out the year following the resignation of Mayor William Boulton.

- First mayor born in Toronto: William Henry Boulton, the city's eighth mayor, was born in York in 1812.
- Number of mayors born inside Toronto's current boundaries: 26
- Number of Irish mayors: Six born in Ireland, and at least eight of Irish ancestry.

TAKE5 FIVE MEMORABLE MAYORS
OF TORONTO

Toronto, at least in its early years (once the boisterous Mackenzie had removed himself from civic politics) did not have history of spectacularly popular (or unpopular) mayors. This may be explained, in part, because the city's mayor was appointed by Council from its members — or elected by only land-owning males — for much of the 1800s. Nevertheless, a few mayors stand out from the ranks of councilmen and and business types who have passed through City Hall over the decades.

1. **The Scapegoat/John Hutchison (mayor 1857, appointed):** Mayor for a only few months, Hutchison resigned after being blamed for a stock market swindle that put thousands of Torontonians out of work. He fled to Montreal, where he died mysteriously three years later. Legend has it that his ghost roams the back stairwells of Toronto's former city hall, now encased inside the St. Lawrence Market, exclaiming his innocence and regret for the long-ago disaster.

2. **Local Hero/Joseph Sheard (mayor 1871–72, appointed):** As a young man Sheard worked as a carpenter for a prominent architect and famously refused to help build the gallows used to hang two leaders of the Rebellion of 1837, Samuel Lount and Peter Matthews. The deed put his own life in danger but made him a hero to the people of Toronto—and they didn't forget it. Sheard became an architect himself and, eventually, when responsible government came in, was elected to council and eventually chosen mayor.

- First mayor to die in office: Samuel McBride (1866–1936), during his second term.
- First Jewish mayor: Nathan Phillips (1892–1976), mayor from 1955 to 1962.

3. Mr. Transition/Thomas "Tommy" Church (mayor 1915–21, elected): Church weathered some of the most traumatic years in the city's history, a period that saw a transition from old Toronto to the dawn of the modern age. His term began during the turbulence of World War I, in which 25,000 Toronto men lost their lives. Two years later women were given the vote, and then, in 1919, the city was devastated by the Spanish influenza pandemic, during which 1,300 people died.

4. Mr. Transportation/Samuel (Sam) McBride (mayor 1928–1929 and 1936, elected): McBride sat on city council for 30 years, was two-time mayor of Toronto and helped create the Toronto Transit Commission. Today Torontonians recall the name mainly because of the *Sam McBride*, one of the ferries christened in 1939 that has taken millions of residents and tourists alike to the Toronto Islands (McBride was among the privileged few who once owned a cottage there).

5. The People's Mayor/David Crombie (mayor 1972–78, elected): Praised and fondly remembered for his reformist ideas for "putting the people first," Crombie made Toronto an extremely livable city. He put a stop to the destruction of Toronto's architectural past and limited the height, at least for a time, of buildings in the downtown core.

FRANCHISE FACTS

Eligibility to vote: Each voter must be 18 or over as of election day, a Canadian citizen and either reside in or own property in Toronto or be the spouse of someone who does. People in jail who have not yet been sentenced can vote; so can the homeless, who can use a shelter, drop-in program or meal program as their address.

ELECTION DAY

Municipal elections are held every four years, on the second Monday in November. Toronto's next election is scheduled for Monday, Nov. 8, 2010.

PROVINCIAL AND FEDERAL REPRESENTATION

Generally, each municipal ward in Toronto is half a federal/provincial riding. There are 22 federal ridings within the city's boundaries. One exception is a tiny piece of eastern Scarborough that now falls into a Pickering-area riding, following the redrawing of electoral boundaries in 2003.

- Toronto MPPs in the Ontario Legislative Assembly: Toronto has 22 of the 107 seats at Queen's Park. Eighteen MPPs were members of the governing Liberals in 2009 and four were NDP members. Eight cabinet ministers represented Toronto ridings.
- Toronto MPs in the House of Commons: In January of 2009, Toronto had 22 of the 308 seats in the House of Commons. Twenty MPs were Liberals, and two (the husband-and-wife team of Jack Layton and Olivia Chow) were NDP.
- Toronto senators: 13 of 105 seats. The prime minister appoints each senator to represent a province but some choose to designate a specific riding or city as their area of concern.

Did you know...

that the civic motto adopted by Toronto's first city council in 1834 was "industry, intelligence, integrity"?

CURRENT ADMINISTRATION

- Mayor: David Miller, 63rd mayor
- Party: A member of the NDP for many years, Miller did not renew his membership in 2007, telling the *Toronto Star*: "I don't want to be in a position where people could accuse me of being partisan. I haven't been. But I want it to be very clear I'm not. My role as mayor inter-governmentally is far too important right now."
- Date sworn in: Dec. 2, 2003; re-elected in November 2006
- Number of councilors: 44
- Number of women: 10
- Number of visible minorities: 4
- Number of staff: 50,184 positions (45,597 permanent, 4,587 temporary)

TAKE 5 MAYOR MILLER'S
FAVOURITE THINGS ABOUT T.O.

Like almost half of Torontonians, Mayor David Miller is an immigrant; he and his mother arrived in Canada from England in 1967 and moved to Toronto in 1981. After earning an economics degree from Harvard and a law degree from U of T, Miller became a partner at Toronto law firm Aird and Berlis. He was elected a Metro councillor in 1994, a City of Toronto councillor in 1997 and mayor in 2003 and 2006. In 2008 he was named chair of the C40 Group of world cities for his role in leading Toronto's environmental agenda and its fight against climate change. Here is Mayor Miller's top five things he loves most about his city.

1. The Humber River pedestrian and cycling bridge.
2. The energy and passion of Toronto's youth.
3. We welcome newcomers and respect our differences.
4. Our big festivals—Pride, Caribana, Toronto International Film.
5. The Toronto Football Club (TFC).

GOVERNMENT DOUGH: WHERE TORONTO GETS ITS CASH

The revenue line of Toronto's 2008 operating budget was $8.2 billion, which broke down as follows:

- Property and related taxes: 41 percent
- Provincial grants and subsidies: 21 percent
- User fees: 15 percent

TAKE 5 MATTHEW BLACKETT'S TOP FIVE
BATTLES TO PRESERVE TORONTO'S SPACES

Matthew Blackett is the publisher of *spacing*, a Toronto-based magazine and blog that covers the joys, obstacles and politics of the urban landscape. Information on the magazine, blog and funky Toronto-themed buttons can be found at www.spacing.ca.

1. **Fort York not moved for the Gardiner Expressway, 1959:** The birthplace of Toronto was in danger of being relocated when plans for the Gardiner Expressway were presented. Fifteen historical groups united as the Associated Historical Societies' Committee of Toronto to defend the fort and fight Metro chair Fred Gardiner. The fort stayed put, and now a new neighbourhood is sprouting up around the largest piece of parkland in the downtown.

2. **Old City Hall saved, 1970s:** When the enormous Eaton Centre plans were announced, old City Hall, one of Toronto's most striking buildings, was reduced to only a clock tower. Again, residents and historical societies banded together to convince the department store and city planners of the worthiness of keeping the iconic building. Eaton's eventually relinquished; the building's roof, exterior and gargoyles were recently restored.

- Other revenues*: 14 percent
- Reserves/reserve funds: 4 percent
- Federal grants and subsidies: 3 percent
- New taxation: 2 percent

(*Interest and investment income, property rental, land transfer tax, etc.)

Source: City of Toronto

3. **Stop the Spadina Expressway, 1971:** Local residents in the Annex neighbourhood banded together to stop Metro Toronto's government from building a major north-south expressway that would cut through the heart of downtown core and the idyllic University of Toronto grounds. A subway line was built along the same route instead. This battle also stopped three other major highways from cutting through vibrant communities.

4. **Island residents refuse eviction, 1980:** The residents of Toronto Islands lease their land from the city government. In 1980 the Metro government wanted to evict the residents to turn the Islands into parks. Residents organized like a local militia with wailing siren alarms so they knew how to react when the sheriff came to deliver the eviction notices. They eventually negotiated new 99-year leases.

5. **Fight to save postering, 2002-07:** The city tried to ban posters on 99 percent of light standards and utility poles while expanding corporate advertising on its own garbage bins and other street furniture. The Toronto Public Space Committee, a local community group, fought the city and eventually helped develop a new policy that allowed community postering for theatre, dog walkers and garage sales to continue on 98 percent of poles while limiting corporate postering campaigns.

TAKE 5 TOP FIVE OCCUPATIONS
BEFORE BECOMING TORONTO'S MAYOR

1. **Lawyer:** 25
2. **Merchant/businessman:** 15
3. **Journalist/publisher:** 8
4. **Doctor, dentist, funeral home director:** 4
5. **Educator:** 3

HOW TORONTO SPENDS ITS DOUGH

- Police Service and Police Board: 24.2 percent
- Debt charges: 12.9 percent
- Fire services: 10.5 percent
- Social services: 8.3 percent
- Shelter, support and housing administration: 7.7 percent
- TTC (including Wheel-Trans): 7.6 percent
- Parks, forestry and recreation: 7.2 percent
- Solid-waste-management services: 5.5 percent
- Transportation services: 5 percent
- Toronto Public Library: 4.7 percent
- Children's services: 2.1 percent
- Emergency medical services: 1.9 percent
- Toronto Public Health: 1.6 percent
- Information and technology: 1.4 percent
- Community Partnerships and Investment Program: 1.3 percent
- Homes for the aged: 1.2 percent
- City council: 0.6 percent
- City planning: 0.4 percent
- Municipal licensing and standards: 0.3 percent
- Toronto building: -0.3 percent
- Other: -4.1 percent

Source: City of Toronto

Bishop Strachan: God in Politics

Never a mayor or even a councilman, John Strachan was arguably the most influential figure in Toronto's history. The standards he put in place as the city's first Anglican bishop—to be the "most British" of Canadian cities—lasted well into the 1950s.

Strachan arrived in York in 1812 to be the rector of the Anglican Church and teacher to the sons of the Family Compact, the powerful group of non-reformist families that ran the politics of the town and the province. He would eventually rise to be the Compact's undisputed leader, a trajectory that began with heroic deeds in 1813.

Many Loyalists in the United States had chosen to move to York following the American War of Independence. The War of 1812, if lost, threatened to change Canada into a republic like its southern neighbour. It was the ideal of God and King above all to which Strachan and his followers held true.

On the morning of April 27, 1813, the American fleet entered York's harbour and began a week-long occupation of the little town. As legend has it, when they started looting his church, Strachan, astride his horse, bellowed "Enough!" and demanded that they leave town and pay pound-for-pound for the damage they had inflicted. American General Henry Dearborn, exhausted from the seasickness he had suffered during the lake voyage, agreed helplessly in front of the imposing figure. And so the myth of John Strachan was born.

In the following years, Strachan was appointed to governing councils and continued to teach and preach, all the while holding steadfast to the belief that God had anointed a monarch to reign over the people, not a president and definitely not a pope. Fiercely anti-Catholic and pro-Anglican, Strachan stood at the helm of the Orange Order that dominated city politics for the next century. As the sons of the elite families grew to become the next generation of Toronto powerbrokers, they continued to look to their former teacher for guidance.

Strachan died in 1867, only months after the new country of Canada was born. His remains are buried beneath the chancel of St. James' Cathedral, the construction of which he oversaw.

BRICKS AND MORTAR SPENDING

In addition to its operating funds, the city also spends money on "bricks and mortar": the building, upgrading and maintaining of community centres, libraries, roads, subways, etc. In 2008 Toronto approved a new five-year (2009 to 2013) capital-budget plan of $11 billion. (Council also declared that after 2013, no new debt will be generated except for TTC expenditures.) Such spending for 2009 totalled $1.637 billion and was funded through a range of sources, including $375 million in financing. The breakdown:

- Toronto Transit Commission: $782 million (48 percent)
- Transportation services: $277 million (17 percent)
- Parks, forestry and recreation: $83 million (5 percent)
- Waterfront revitalization: $66 million (4 percent)
- Fleet services (vehicles owned by the city): $49 million (3 percent)
- Facilities and real estate: $45 million (3 percent)
- Police Service: $37 million (2 percent)
- GO Transit: $20 million (1 percent)
- Other: $278 million (17 percent)

Source: City of Toronto

DEBT

Toronto is currently in debt to the tune of $2.1 billion. In 2008, for the first time since amalgamation, its operating budget was balanced.

Did you know. . .

that not only was William Lyon Mackenzie the first mayor of Toronto but he was also the first mayor elected in Ontario? The staunch opponent of the elitism of the ruling class, Mackenzie struggled with debt all his life yet reduced his own proposed salary from £250 to £100 per year. The price on his head following his failed Upper Canada Rebellion three years later was £1,000—10 times his mayoral salary.

TAKE 5 FIVE CONTROVERSIAL QUOTES
FROM MAYOR MEL LASTMAN

Mayor Mel held the top post in North York for 25 years before becoming Toronto's first post-amalgamation mayor. Voters from the old suburbs voted for him in high numbers, fearing that the opposing candidate, Barbara Hall, was too "downtown." An immensely popular mayor and former furniture store owner—his furniture chain was called Bad Boy; he called himself the "Bad Boy" and once went to the Arctic to try to sell a refrigerator to an Eskimo as a publicity stunt—Lastman was a tireless salesman for Toronto who nevertheless was known for opening his mouth and inserting his foot (sometimes both feet). These five controversial statements he made while in office will give you the idea.

1. *"Too many parents think all they have to do is give birth and walk away."* Said at a meeting of the Federation of Canadian Municipalities in 1979. It was later revealed that Lastman's children by his mistress were living in poverty at the time.

2. *"You will never be mayor of this city because you say stupid and dumb things!"* Addressed to David Miller in May of 2002; Miller was elected mayor in 2003.

3. *"What the hell would I want to go to a place like Mombasa for? Snakes just scare the hell out of me. I'm sort of scared about going, but the wife is really nervous. I just see myself in a pot of boiling water with all these natives dancing around me."* Said in June of 2001 before leaving for a trip to Kenya in support of Toronto's 2008 Olympics bid.

4. *"Take a look at Yonge Street, it looks like a flea market. It's the longest street in the world but it looks like hell. There's a big store there that hangs jeans and ladies clothes outside and that's bulls#!t. This is Yonge Street, it's got to have a touch of class. I want this to be a great city."* Media interview, 1998.

5. *"[There are] no homeless in North York."* Said during his 1997 bid to become the first mayor of the amalgamated Toronto, a day before a homeless woman was found dead at a North York gas station.

TOTAL PROPERTY TAXES AND UTILITY CHARGES

If we take, for comparison purposes, a 25- to 30-year-old detached, three-bedroom, 1,200 sq. ft. bungalow on a 6,000 sq. ft. lot, Toronto emerges with the third-highest property taxes and utility charges in the country.

- Brampton $4,987
- Hamilton $4,807
- **Toronto**   **$4,744**
- Ottawa $4,680
- Saskatoon $4,671
- Vancouver $4,506
- Edmonton $4,133
- Saint John $3,991
- Halifax $3,983
- Calgary $3,973
- Montreal $3,815
- Winnipeg $3,529
- Medicine Hat $3,516
- St. John's $3,328

**Utility charges include telephone, power, water, sewer, land drainage and garbage collection.

Source: City of Edmonton, Planning and Development Department

TURNOUT IN MUNICIPAL ELECTIONS POST-AMALGAMATION

The first post-amalgamation vote in Toronto attracted almost half of the eligible population to the polls. The mayor's race was a battle between North York Mayor Mel Lastman and Barbara Hall, mayor of the former City of Toronto (Lastman won). The mayoralty race was also the focus of the 2003 election, which started with five high-profile candidates and ended as a race between David Miller and John Tory, who went on to become leader of the Ontario Conservatives.

- 1997: 760,589 voters, or 45.6 percent of eligible voters
- 2000: 626,759 voters, or 36.1 percent of eligible voters
- 2003: 699,492 voters, or 38.3 percent of eligible voters

- 2006: 597,754 voters, or 39.2 percent of eligible voters

Source: City of Toronto Elections Office

SALARIES AND BUDGETS

Mayor David Miller's 2008 salary: $163,040
Each of the 44 city councillors' salaries: $96,805
Mayor's total office budget: $2,601,100
Total cost of staff: $2,251,300
Office perks per councillor: Three support staff, parking space and $53,100 for office expenses

WOMEN IN POLITICS

In 1850 propertied women were given the right to vote for school trustees. Women gained the right to vote provincially in 1917 and federally in 1918 (except for aboriginal women). All of these milestones were achieved through the hard work of the women's suffrage movement, no small part of which unfolded in Toronto.

In 1876 Toronto feminist Dr. Emily Stowe founded the Toronto Women's Literary Club, which became the Canadian Women's Suffrage Association in 1883. A decade later, 1,500 women attended a meeting in Toronto and founded the National Council of Women of Canada. Its goal was to improve the status of immigrant women, the lot of women in jails and factories and gain the vote.

Soon the Women's Christian Temperance Union, which had been founded in Toronto in 1875 to stamp out the evils of alcohol, threw its forces behind the group. And in 1892, long before women gained the vote, Torontonians elected a woman for the first time—three, in fact, to serve on the Board of Education.

Toronto's first female city councillor was Constance Hamilton, who was elected in 1920. In the 1945 provincial election, the first women ever elected to the Ontario Legislature, Rae Luckock and Agnes Macphail, became MPPs for the Toronto wards of Bracondale and York East, respectively. The first woman elected to represent Toronto in the federal government was Margaret Aitken; she represented York-Humber for eight years beginning in 1953.

Toronto has had two female mayors: June Rowlands (1992–94) and Barbara Hall (1995–97).

NO BARENAKED LADIES

In 1991 June Rowlands became first woman to win a Toronto mayoralty race, defeating Jack Layton, following a long career of municipal service. She may best be remembered by a certain fraction of Torontonians for banning the rock band The Barenaked Ladies from playing at the 1991 New Year's Eve concert in Nathan Phillips Square. (While the group's performance was struck from the roster, the resulting publicity was a boon for them.) Some sources say it was a staffer who made the call, but many saw the incident as a demonstration of how Rowlands was out of touch with the times; her supporters say her decision protested the objectification of women. She did not win re-election.

PERENNIAL CANDIDATES

A handful of perennial candidates have run for office in Toronto. Two of the most notable were Kevin Clarke and the late Ben Kerr. Clarke, who has a long history of homelessness and street preaching, first ran for mayor of East York in 1994. He ran provincially in 1995, 1996, 2001 and 2007, then federally in 1997. He also ran for mayor of Toronto in 2000, 2003 and 2006, as well as in councillor byelections in 1998, 2001 and 2006. He has not yet been elected.

Kerr ran for mayor in every municipal election from 1985 to 2003. A well-known street busker who often performed at the corner of Yonge and Bloor, he was a vehement anti-smoking campaigner and an

Did you know. . .

that Toronto city council voted to decriminalize prostitution in 1995, but the federal government quickly nixed the proposal?

advocate for cayenne pepper as a health enhancer. In 2007 Toronto city council named a street after him in the Danforth and Jones area, where he had lived for 25 years.

TAKE 5 FIVE SIGNIFICANT
POLITICAL BUILDINGS AND SITES

1. **Old City Hall (60 Queen St. West):** Now a courthouse, this Romanesque building was Toronto city council headquarters from 1899 to 1965. Designed by Edward James Lennox, the designing hand behind Casa Loma and the King Edward Hotel, it was the largest municipal building in North America when it was completed. It features stone gargoyles and carvings outside, stained glass and murals inside and cost $2.5 million to erect.

2. **Toronto City Hall (100 Queen St. West):** The current City Hall, just west of old City Hall, opened in 1965. Finnish architect Viljo Revell's modern sculptural design placed the round council chambers—referred to by some Torontonians as the "spaceship"—between two curved towers of different heights. It cost about $31 million to build.

3. **Metro Hall (55 John St.):** Opened in 1992 as the seat of government for the Metropolitan level of government complete with council chambers, the 27-storey post-modern tower is the centrepiece of the Metro Centre. The City of Toronto took over the building after amalgamation.

4. **Parliament buildings 1, 2, 3:** Before Ottawa became the capital of Canada in 1865, Toronto often hosted the federal parliament, alternating with Montreal. The first buildings, at Front and Parliament, were burned during the American occupation of 1813. New structures rebuilt on the site in 1820 were destroyed by fire four years later. The third set, built farther west on Front Street near Simcoe in 1832, became home to the provincial legislature following Confederation (CBC headquarters now sits on that site).

5. **Ontario legislature:** Opened in April of 1893, and built at a cost of about $1.25 million, these pink sandstone Romanesque structures are often called Queen's Park, which more accurately refers to their setting. Named after Queen Victoria and established in 1860, the surrounding green space is one of Canada's earliest urban parks.

They said it

Weblinks

Toronto Government: An Overview

www.toronto.ca/committees/pdf/committee-structure-org-chart.pdf
A chart of the City of Toronto's governing structure, with links to the various city council committees. It's useful for understanding how decisions are made and who makes them.

Community Social Planning Council of Toronto

http://socialplanningtoronto.org
CSPC-T is a non-profit organization engaged in neighbourhood and city-wide social planning and related activities. The website provides a means for activists and community members to keep abreast of social and political issues facing communities.

Did you know. . .

that China, Germany, Great Britain, India, the United States and 87 other countries maintain consular offices in Toronto?

Did you know. . .

that in 1965, after city council refused to purchase abstract art with public funds, Mayor Phil Givens personally campaigned to raise the $120,000 needed to buy Henry Moore's *The Archer*, which has graced New City Hall's Nathan Phillips Square since 1966? The issue led to Givens' defeat in his 1966 re-election bid.